MICROSOFT EXCEL

SHORTCUT KEYS AND FORMULAS

KABIR DAS

ISBN 979-888546040-8

Contents

CHAPTER ONE

Microsoft Excel

Definition

Excel definition: a software program created by Microsoft that uses spreadsheets to organize numbers and data with formulas and functions. Excel analysis is ubiquitous around the world and used by businesses of all sizes to perform financial analysis.

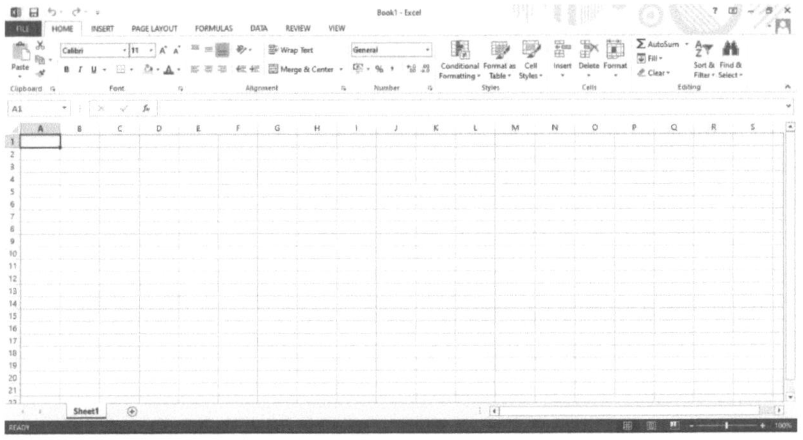

fig: Microsoft excel 2013

The main uses of Excel include:

- Data entry
- Data management
- Accounting
- Financial analysis
- Charting and graphing
- Programming
- Time management
- Task management
- Financial modeling
- Customer relationship management (CRM)
- Almost anything that needs to be organized!

What is Microsoft Excel?

Microsoft Excel is a spreadsheet program used to record and analyze numerical and statistical data. Microsoft Excel provides multiple features to perform various operations like calculations, pivot tables, graph tools, macro programming, etc. It is compatible with multiple OS like Windows, macOS, Android and iOS.

A Excel spreadsheet can be understood as a collection of columns and rows that form a table. Alphabetical letters are usually assigned to columns, and numbers are usually assigned to rows. The point where a column and a row meet is called a cell. The address of a cell is given by the letter representing the column and the number representing a row.

Why Should I Learn Microsoft Excel?

We all deal with numbers in one way or the other. We all have daily expenses which we pay for from the monthly income that we earn. For one to spend wisely, they will need to know their income vs. expenditure. Microsoft Excel comes in handy when we want to record, analyze and store such numeric data. Let's illustrate this using the following image.

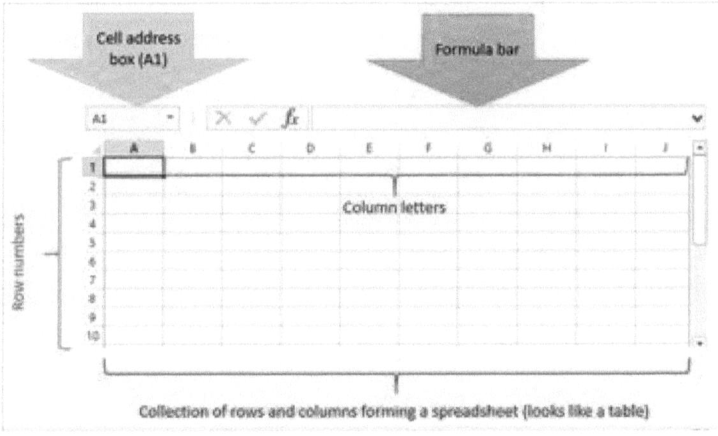

fig: Excel Formatting data

Where can I get Microsoft Excel?

There are number of ways in which you can get Microsoft Excel. You can buy it from a hardware computer shop that also sells software. Microsoft Excel is part of the Microsoft Office suite of programs. Alternatively, you can download it from the Microsoft website but you will have to buy the license key.

In this Microsoft Excel tutorial, we are going to cover the following topics about MS Excel.

- How to Open Microsoft Excel?
- Understanding the Ribbon
- Understanding the worksheet
- Customization Microsoft Excel Environment
- Important Excel shortcuts

How to Open Microsoft Excel?

Running Excel is not different from running any other Windows program. If you are running Windows with a GUI like (Windows XP, Vista, and 7) follow the following steps.

- Click on start menu
- Point to all programs
- Point to Microsoft Excel
- Click on Microsoft Excel

Alternatively, you can also open it from the start menu if it has been added there. You can also open it from the desktop shortcut if you have created one.

Follow the following steps to run Excel on Windows 8 and 10.

- Click on start menu
- Search for Excel N.B. even before you even typing, all programs starting with what you have typed will be listed.
- Click on Microsoft Excel

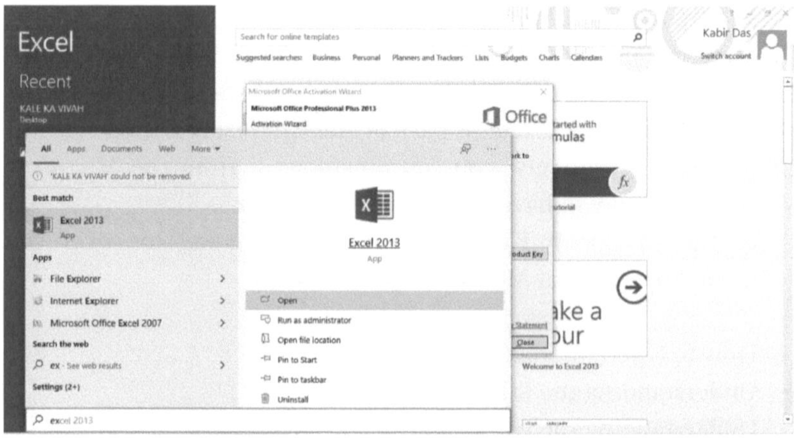

fig: Run Excel on Windows 8 and 10.

Understanding the Ribbon

The ribbon provides shortcuts to commands in Excel. A command is an action that the user performs. An example of a command is creating a new document, printing a documenting, etc.

The image below shows the ribbon used in Excel 2013.

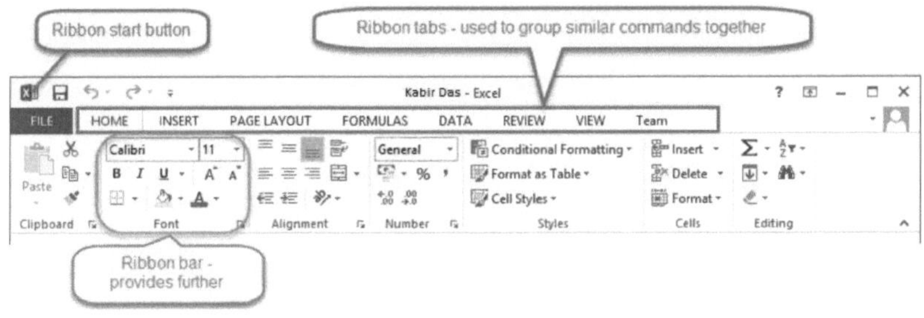

fig: toolbar

Ribbon components explained

Ribbon start button – it is used to access commands i.e. creating new documents, saving existing work, printing, accessing the options for customizing Excel, etc.

Ribbon tabs – the tabs are used to group similar commands together. The home tab is used for basic commands such as formatting the data to make it more presentable, sorting and finding specific data within the spreadsheet.

Ribbon bar – the bars are used to group similar commands together. As an example, the Alignment ribbon bar is used to group all the commands that are used to align data together.

Understanding the worksheet (Rows and Columns, Sheets, Workbooks)

A worksheet is a collection of rows and columns. When a row and a column meet, they form a cell. Cells are used to record data. Each cell is uniquely identified using a cell address. Columns are usually labelled with letters while rows are usually numbers.

A workbook is a collection of worksheets. By default, a workbook has three cells in Excel. You can delete or add more sheets to suit your requirements. By default, the sheets are named Sheet1, Sheet2 and so on and so forth. You can rename the sheet names to more meaningful names i.e. Daily Expenses, Monthly Budget, etc.

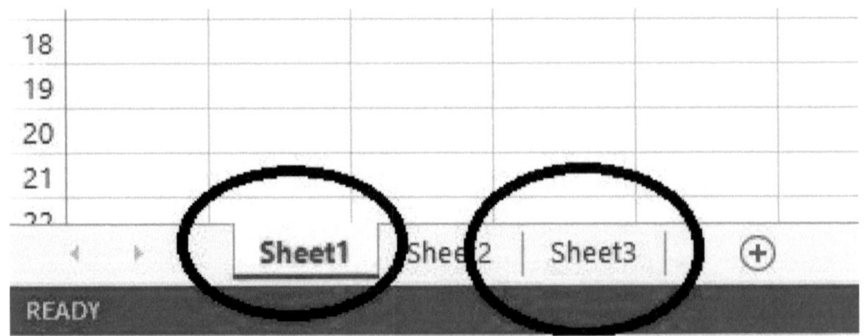

fig: sheet detail or Double click to rename.

Customization Microsoft Excel Environment

Personally I like the black colour, so my excel theme looks blackish. Your favourite colour could be blue, and you too can make your theme colour look blue-like. If you are not a programmer, you may not want to include ribbon tabs i.e. developer. All this is made possible via customizations. In this sub-section, we are going to look at;

- Customization the ribbon
- Setting the colour theme
- Settings for formulas
- Proofing settings
- Save settings

Customization of ribbon

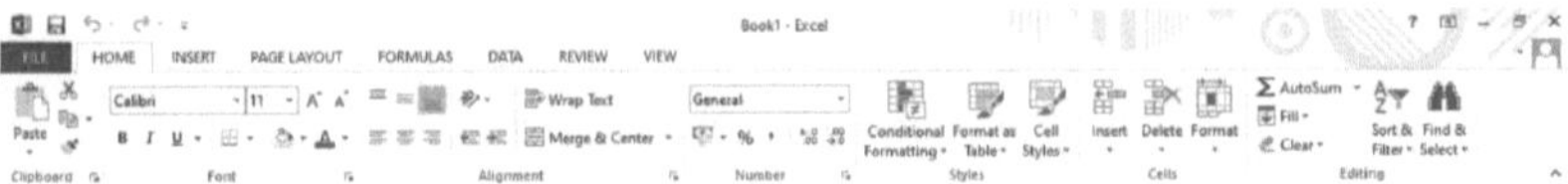

The above image shows the default ribbon in Excel 2013. Let's start with customization the ribbon, suppose you do not wish to see some of the tabs on the ribbon, or you would like to add some tabs that are missing such as the developer tab. You can use the options window to achieve this.

- Click on the ribbon start button
- Select options from the drop down menu. You should be able to see an Excel Options dialog window
- Select the customize ribbon option from the left-hand side panel as shown below

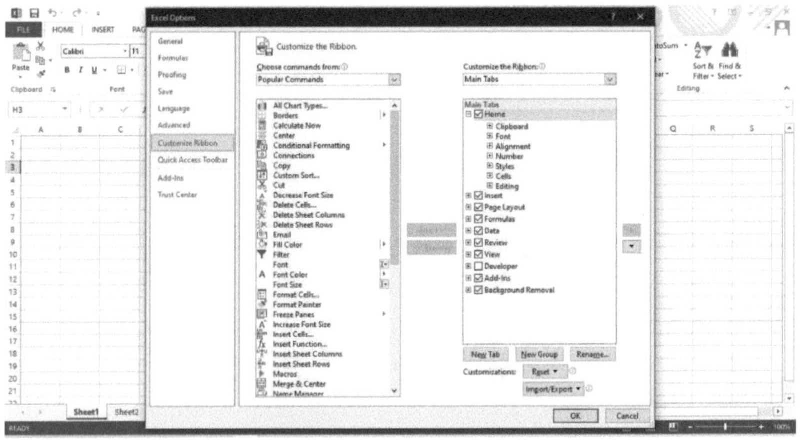

fig:Customize rebbon

- On your right-hand side, remove the check marks from the tabs that you do not wish to see on the ribbon. For this example, we have removed Page Layout, Review, and View tab.
- Click on the "OK" button when you are done.

Your ribbon will look as follows

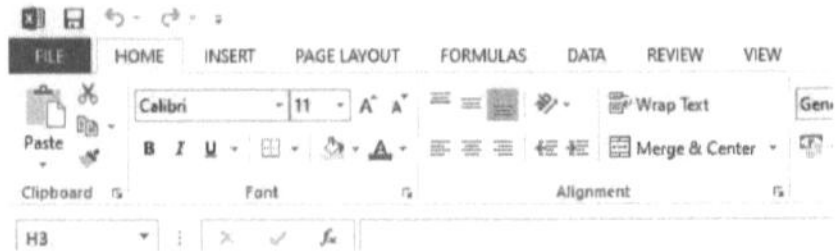

Adding custom tabs to the ribbon

You can also add your own tab, give it a custom name and assign commands to it. Let's add a tab to the ribbon with the text KD.

1. Right click on the ribbon and select Customize the Ribbon. The dialogue window shown above will appear
2. Click on new tab button as illustrated in the animated image below
3. Select the newly created tab
4. Click on Rename button
5. Give it a name of Guru99
6. Select the New Group (Custom) under Guru99 tab as shown in the image below
7. Click on Rename button and give it a name of My Commands
8. Let's now add commands to my ribbon bar
9. The commands are listed on the middle panel
10. Select All chart types command and click on Add button
11. Click on OK

Your ribbon will look as follows

Colour theme

To set the color-theme for your Excel sheet you have to go to Excel ribbon, and click on à File àOption command. It will open a window where you have to follow the following steps.

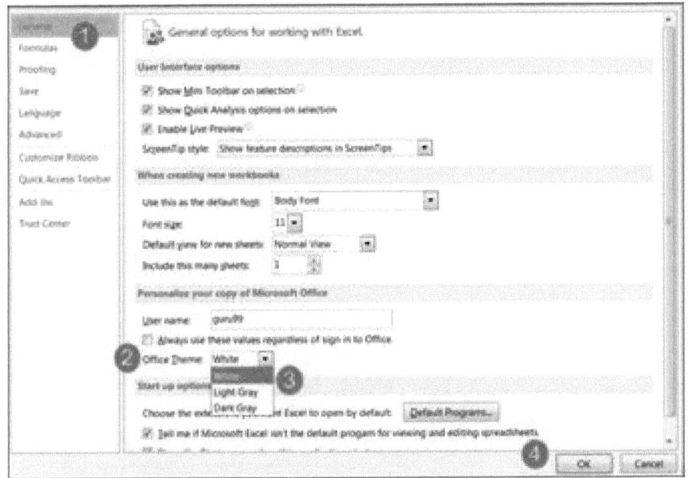

fig: **colour theme**

1. The general tab on the left-hand panel will be selected by default.
2. Look for colour scheme under General options for working with Excel
3. Click on the colour scheme drop-down list and select the desired colour
4. Click on OK button

Formulas

This option allows you to define how Excel behaves when you are working with formulas. You can use it to set options i.e.

autocomplete when entering formulas, change the cell referencing style and use numbers for both columns and rows and other options.

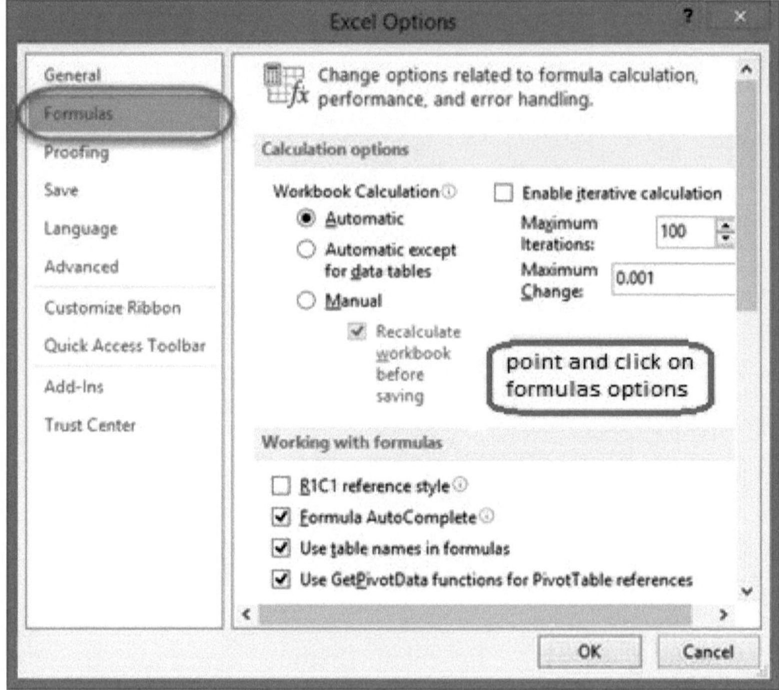

fig: Formulas

If you want to activate an option, click on its check box. If you want to deactivate an option, remove the mark from the checkbox. You can this option from the Options dialogue window under formulas tab from the left-hand side panel

Proofing settings

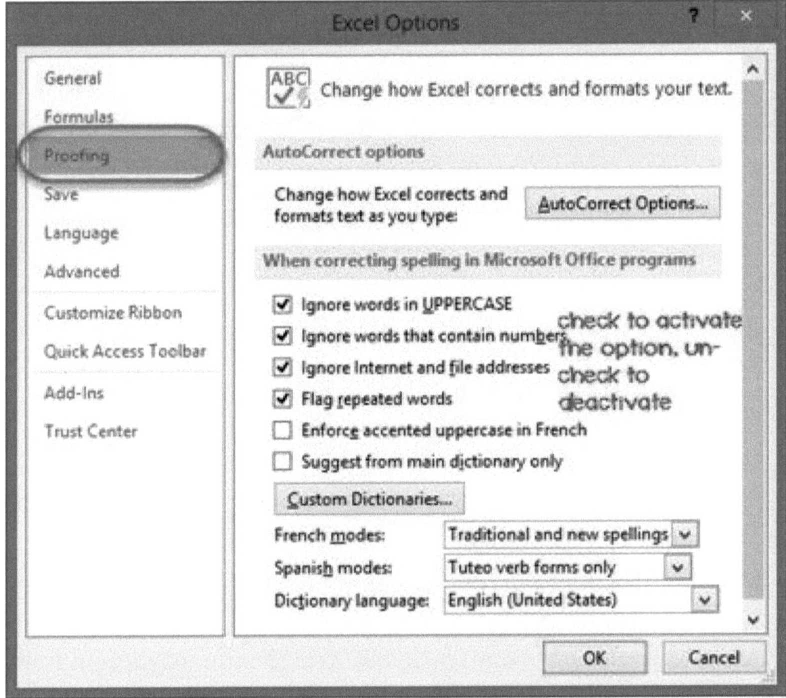

fig: Proofing

This option manipulates the entered text entered into excel. It allows setting options such as the dictionary language that should be used when checking for wrong spellings, suggestions from the dictionary, etc. You can this option from the options dialogue window under the proofing tab from the left-hand side panel

Save settings

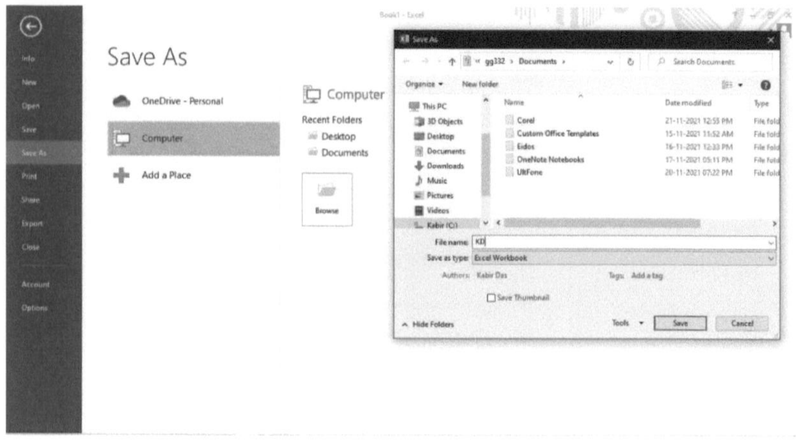

fig: save

This option allows you to define the default file format when saving files, enable auto recovery in case your computer goes off before you could save your work, etc. You can use this option from the Options dialogue window under save tab from the left-hand side panel

Important Excel shortcuts

- **Ctrl + P**
  used to open the print dialogue window
- **Ctrl + N**
  creates a new workbook
- **Ctrl + S**
  saves the current workbook
- **Ctrl + C**
  copy contents of current select
- **Ctrl + V**
  paste data from the clipboard

- **SHIFT + F3**
  displays the function insert dialog window
- **SHIFT + F11**
  Creates a new worksheet
- **F2**
  Check formula and cell range covered

Best Practices when working with Microsoft Excel

1. Save workbooks with backward compatibility in mind. If you are not using the latest features in higher versions of Excel, you should save your files in 2003 *.xls format for backwards compatibility
2. **Use description names for columns and worksheets in a workbook**
3. **Avoid working with complex formulas with many variables.** Try to break them down into small managed results that you can use to build on
4. **Use built-in functions whenever you can instead of writing your own formulas**

Summary

- Introduction of MS Excel : Microsoft Excel is a powerful spreadsheet program used to record, manipulate, store numeric data and it can be customized to match your preferences
- The ribbon is used to access various commands in Excel
- The options dialogue window allows you to customize a number of items i.e. the ribbon, formulas, proofing, save, etc.

CHAPTER TWO

Basic and advance Shortcut keys of Excel

Basic and advance shortcut keys of Excel:-

1. **Ctrl + N**: To create a new workbook.
2. **Ctrl + O**: To open a saved workbook.
3. **Ctrl + S**: To save a workbook.
4. **Ctrl + A**: To select all the contents in a workbook.
5. **Ctrl + B**: To turn highlighted cells bold.
6. **Ctrl + C**: To copy cells that are highlighted.
7. **Ctrl + D**: To fill the selected cell with the content of the cell right above.
8. **Ctrl + F**: To search for anything in a workbook.
9. **Ctrl + G**: To jump to a certain area with a single command.
10. **Ctrl + H**: To find and replace cell contents.
11. **Ctrl + I**: To italicise cell contents.
12. **Ctrl + K**: To insert a hyperlink in a cell.
13. **Ctrl + L**: To open the create table dialog box.
14. **Ctrl + P**: To print a workbook.
15. **Ctrl + R**: To fill the selected cell with the content of the cell on the left.
16. **Ctrl + U**: To underline highlighted cells.
17. **Ctrl + V**: To paste anything that was copied.
18. **Ctrl + W**: To close your current workbook.
19. **Ctrl + Z**: To undo the last action.

20. **Ctrl** + **1**: To format the cell contents.
21. **Ctrl** + **5**: To put a strikethrough in a cell.
22. **Ctrl** + **8**: To show the outline symbols.
23. **Ctrl** + **9**: To hide a row.
24. **Ctrl** + **0**: To hide a column.
25. **Ctrl** + **Shift** + :: To enter the current time in a cell.
26. **Ctrl** + ;: To enter the current date in a cell.
27. **Ctrl** + `: To change the view from displaying cell values to formulas.
28. **Ctrl** + ‘: To copy the formula from the cell above.
29. **Ctrl** + -: To delete columns or rows.
30. **Ctrl** + **Shift** + =: To insert columns and rows.
31. **Ctrl** + **Shift** + ~: To switch between displaying Excel formulas or their values in cell.
32. **Ctrl** + **Shift** + @: To apply time formatting.
33. **Ctrl** + **Shift** + !: To apply comma formatting.
34. **Ctrl** + **Shift** + $: To apply currency formatting.
35. **Ctrl** + **Shift** + #: To apply date formatting.
36. **Ctrl** + **Shift** + %: To apply percentage formatting.
37. **Ctrl** + **Shift** + &: To place borders around the selected cells.
38. **Ctrl** + **Shift** + _: To remove a border.
39. **Ctrl** + -: To delete a selected row or column.
40. **Ctrl** + **Spacebar**: To select an entire column.
41. **Ctrl** + **Shift** + **Spacebar**: To select an entire workbook.
42. **Ctrl** + **Home**: To redirect to cell A1.
43. **Ctrl** + **Shift** + **Tab**: To switch to the previous workbook.
44. **Ctrl** + **Shift** + **F**: To open the fonts menu under format cells.
45. **Ctrl** + **Shift** + **O**: To select the cells containing comments.
46. **Ctrl** + **Drag**: To drag and copy a cell or to a duplicate worksheet.
47. **Ctrl** + **Shift** + **Drag**: To drag and insert copy.
48. **Ctrl** + **Up arrow**: To go to the top most cell in a current column.
49. **Ctrl** + **Down arrow**: To jump to the last cell in a current column.
50. **Ctrl** + **Right arrow**: To go to the last cell in a selected row.
51. **Ctrl** + **Left arrow**: To jump back to the first cell in a selected row.
52. **Ctrl** + **End**: To go to the last cell in a workbook.

53. **Alt + Page down**: To move the screen towards the right.
54. **Alt + Page Up**: To move the screen towards the left.
55. **Ctrl + F2**: To open the print preview window.
56. **Ctrl + F1**: To expand or collapse the ribbon.
57. **Alt**: To open the access keys.
58. **Tab**: Move to the next cell.
59. **Alt + F + T**: To open the options.
60. **Alt + Down arrow**: To activate filters for cells.
61. **F2**: To edit a cell.
62. **F3**: To paste a cell name if the cells have been named.
63. **Shift + F2**: To add or edit a cell comment.
64. **Alt + H + H**: To select a fill colour.
65. **Alt + H + B**: To add a border.
66. **Ctrl + 9**: To hide the selected rows.
67. **Ctrl + 0**: To hide the selected columns.
68. **Esc**: To cancel an entry.
69. **Enter**: To complete the entry in a cell and move to the next one.
70. **Shift + Right arrow**: To extend the cell selection to the right.
71. **Shift + Left arrow**: To extend the cell selection to the left.
72. **Shift + Space**: To select the entire row.
73. **Page up/ down**: To move the screen up or down.
74. **Alt + H**: To go to the Home tab in Ribbon.
75. **Alt + N**: To go to the Insert tab in Ribbon.
76. **Alt + P**: To go to the Page Layout tab in Ribbon.
77. **Alt + M**: To go to the Formulas tab in Ribbon.
78. **Alt + A**: To go to the Data tab in Ribbon.
79. **Alt + R**: To go to the Review tab in Ribbon.
80. **Alt + W**: To go to the View tab in Ribbon.
81. **Alt + Y**: To open the Help tab in Ribbon.
82. **Alt + Q**: To quickly jump to search.
83. **Alt + Enter**: To start a new line in a current cell.
84. **Shift + F3**: To open the Insert function dialog box.
85. **F9**: To calculate workbooks.
86. **Shift + F9**: To calculate an active workbook.
87. **Ctrl + Alt + F9**: To force calculate all workbooks.

88. **Ctrl + F3**: To open the name manager.
89. **Ctrl + Shift + F3**: To create names from values in rows and columns.
90. **Ctrl + Alt + +**: To zoom in inside a workbook.
91. **Ctrl + Alt +**: To zoom out inside a workbook.
92. **Alt + 1**: To turn on Autosave.
93. **Alt + 2**: To save a workbook.
94. **Alt + F + E**: To export your workbook.
95. **Alt + F + Z**: To share your workbook.
96. **Alt + F + C**: To close and save your workbook.
97. **Alt or F11**: To turn key tips on or off.
98. **Alt + Y + W**: To know what's new in Microsoft Excel.
99. **F1**: To open Microsoft Excel help.
100. **Ctrl + F4**: To close Microsoft Excel.

Q:- How to Write Your Own Keyboard Shortcuts in Microsoft Excel.

Create Custom Excel Shortcuts (2 Ways)

Applies to: Microsoft® Excel® 2013, 2016, 2019 and 365 (Windows)

Microsoft Excel has many built-in shortcuts as well as the ability to navigate and select in the Ribbon using the keyboard. However, you may also want to write your own keyboard shortcuts for specific commands.

Unfortunately, Excel doesn't offer a keyboard assignments command similar to the one available in Microsoft Word. In Word, you can assign keyboard shortcuts through the Options command on the File tab. In the Customize Ribbon category, there is a Keyboard Shortcuts Customize button that is not available in Excel. So, you have a couple of options in Excel. You can add buttons to the Quick Access toolbar (which are automatically assigned Alt shortcuts) or you can write a macro using the Macro Recorder.

1. Creating a keyboard shortcut by customizing the Quick Access Toolbar

To customize the Quick Access Toolbar and create keyboard

shortcuts:

- Click the File tab in the Ribbon and then click on Options.
- Click the Quick Access Toolbar category on the left.
- From the drop-down menu under Choose commands from, select All Commands.
- Click the button you want to add.
- Click Add.
- Continue adding buttons.
- If you want to re-order buttons, click the button in the Customize Quick Access toolbar pane on the right and click the Move Up or Move Down arrow buttons.
- Click Close.

Commands appear in the Excel Options dialog box:

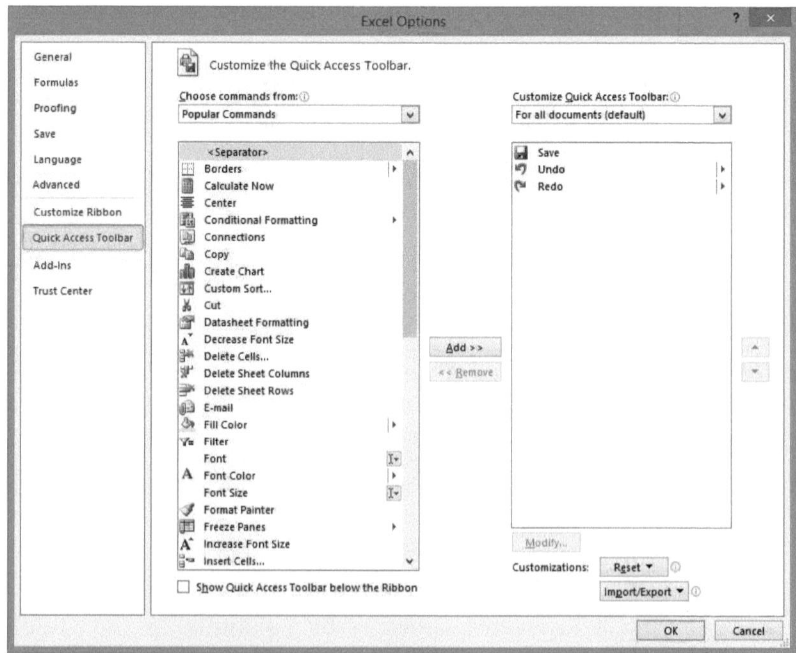

Once you have added the desired buttons, Excel assigns keyboard shortcuts automatically to the buttons based on the order in the Quick Access Toolbar. For example, the first button can be accessed by pressing Alt and then 1, the second button by pressing Alt and then 2 and so on.

2. Creating a macro with a keyboard shortcut using the Macro Recorder

You can also add a keyboard shortcut by recording a macro. In Excel, you can record a macro to automate specific actions and you can assign a keyboard shortcut to the macro. To keep things simple, we'll use the Record Macro button on the View tab in the Ribbon.

You'll be using the Record Macro dialog (below) to create keyboard shortcuts:

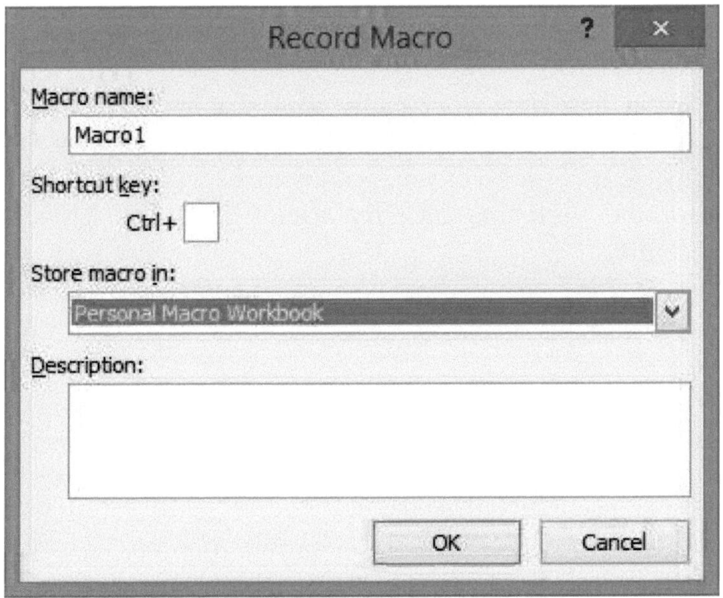

To create a macro and assign a keyboard shortcut:

1. Open the file you want to use or create a new workbook.
2. Click the View tab in the Ribbon.
3. Click Macros and select Record Macro. A dialog box appears.
4. Under Macro Name, name the macro (no more than 255 characters and do not include spaces or begin with a number or an underscore).
5. Under Shortcut key, enter a keyboard shortcut. For example, type Shift + H (this would assign Control + Shift + H as the shortcut). By adding Shift, you are less likely to create the same shortcut as a built-in Excel shortcut.
6. Under Store macro in, choose This Workbook, New Workbook or Personal Macro Workbook. For global shortcuts, save the macro in the Personal Macro Workbook which is launched on startup and is hidden by default. If you store a macro in another workbook, it will need to be open to run the macro.
7. Under Description, you can enter a description.
8. Click OK.
9. Perform the actions you want to record. For example, click Paste on the Home tab, choose Paste Special and then click on Values in the dialog box. All of your actions are being recorded.
10. Click the View tab, click on Macros and then select Stop Recording.
11. Try pressing the keyboard shortcut combination that you assigned to run the macro.

When you use the Macro Recorder, Excel writes the code for the macro using VBA (Visual Basic for Applications). If a macro you created in the Personal Macro Workbook doesn't work as expected, you will probably want to delete it.

To delete a macro that is stored in the Personal Macro Workbook, you will need to unhide the workbook first. To unhide the Personal Macro Workbook, click Unhide on the View tab, click Personal and click OK. To delete a macro, click Macros on the View tab and choose View Macros. Click on the macro you want to delete and click Delete. Be sure to hide the Personal Macro Workbook again using Hide on the View tab.

If you have displayed the Developer tab in the Ribbon, Record Macro as well as other useful buttons appear in this tab as well.

CHAPTER THREE

Basic Formulas

Basic Excel Formulas Guide

Mastering the basic Excel formulas is critical for beginners to become highly proficient in financial analysis. Microsoft Excel is considered the industry standard piece of software in data analysis. Microsoft's spreadsheet program also happens to be one of the most preferred software by investment bankers and financial analysts in data processing, financial modelling, and presentation. This guide will provide an overview and list of basic Excel functions.

Basic Terms in Excel

There are two basic ways to perform calculations in Excel: Formulas and Functions.

1. **Formulas**
   In Excel, a formula is an expression that operates on values in a range of cells or a cell. For example, =A1+A2+A3, which finds the sum of the range of values from cell A1 to cell A3.
2. **Functions**
   Functions are predefined formulas in Excel. They eliminate laborious manual entry of formulas while giving them human-friendly names. For example: =SUM(A1:A3). The function sums all the values from A1 to A3.

Five Time-saving Ways to Insert Data into Excel

When analyzing data, there are five common ways of inserting basic Excel formulas. Each strategy comes with its own advantages.

Therefore, before diving further into the main formulas, we'll clarify those methods, so you can create your preferred workflow earlier on.

1.) Simple insertion: Typing a formula inside the cell

- Typing a formula in a cell or the formula bar is the most straightforward method of inserting basic Excel formulas. The process usually starts by typing an equal sign, followed by the name of an Excel function.
- Excel is quite intelligent in that when you start typing the name of the function, a pop-up function hint will show. It's from this list you'll select your preference. However, don't press the Enter key. Instead, press the Tab key so that you can continue to insert other options. Otherwise, you may find yourself with an invalid name error, often as '#NAME?'. To fix it, just re-select the cell, and go to the formula bar to complete your function.

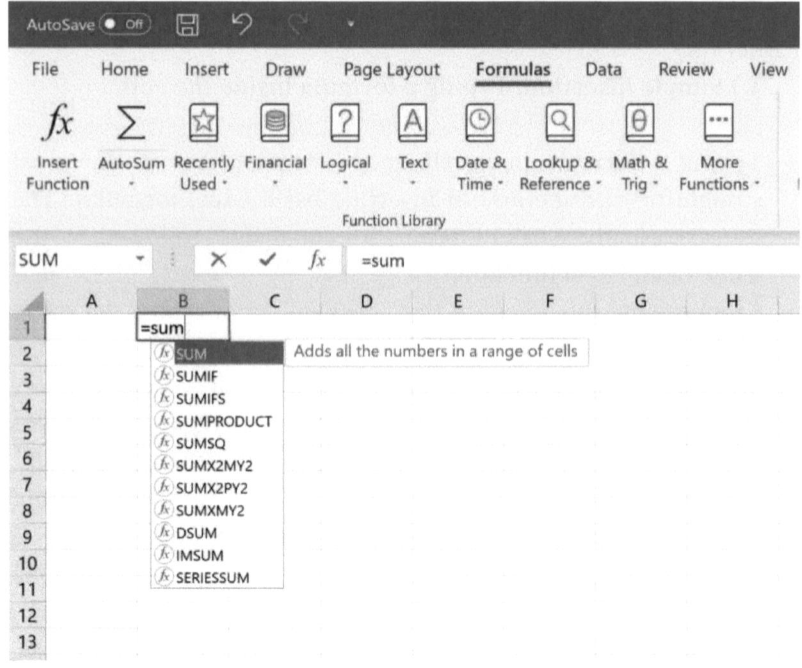

2.) Using Insert Function Option from Formulas Tab

- If you want full control of your functions insertion, using the Excel Insert Function dialogue box is all you ever need. To achieve this, go to the Formulas tab and select the first menu labeled Insert Function. The dialogue box will contain all the functions you need to complete your financial analysis.

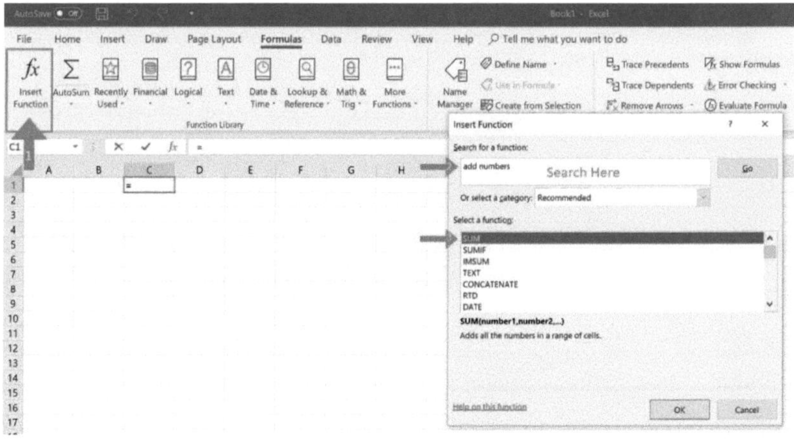

3.) Selecting a Formula from One of the Groups in Formula Tab

- This option is for those who want to delve into their favorite functions quickly. To find this menu, navigate to the Formulas tab and select your preferred group. Click to show a sub-menu filled with a list of functions. From there, you can select your preference. However, if you find your preferred group is not on the tab, click on the More Functions option – it's probably just hidden there.

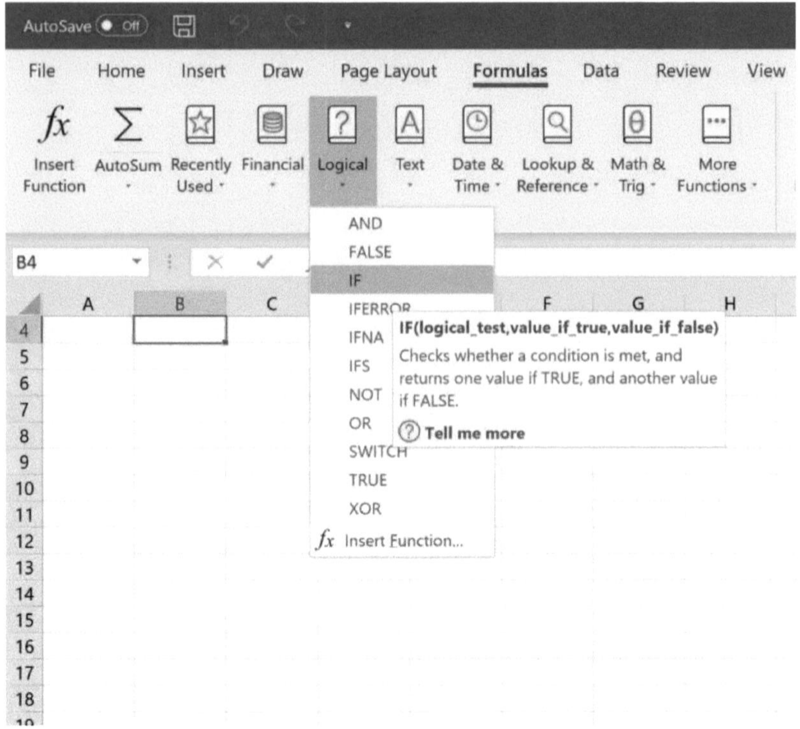

4.) Using AutoSum Option

- For quick and everyday tasks, the AutoSum function is your go-to option. So, navigate to the Home tab, in the far-right corner, and click the AutoSum option. Then click the caret to show other hidden formulas. This option is also available in the Formulas tab first option after the Insert Function option.

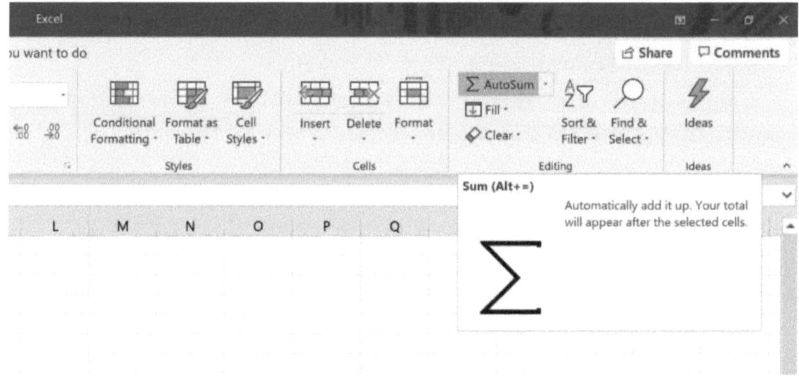

5.) Quick Insert: Use Recently Used Tabs

- If you find re-typing your most recent formula a monotonous task, then use the Recently Used menu. It's on the Formulas tab, a third menu option just next to AutoSum.

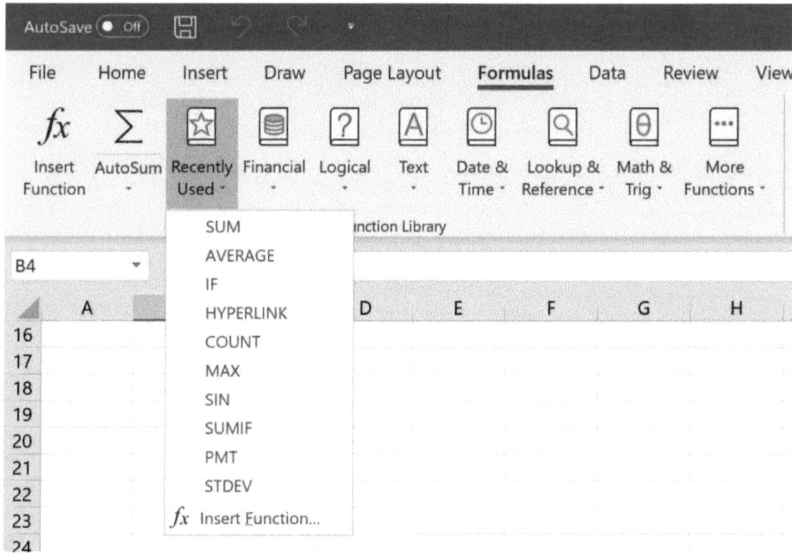

Basic Excel Formulas For Your Workflow

Since you're now able to insert your preferred formulas and function correctly, let's check some fundamental Excel functions to get you started.

1. SUM

- The SUM function is the first must-know formula in Excel. It usually aggregates values from a selection of columns or rows from your selected range.
  =SUM(number1, [number2], ...)
  Example:
  =SUM(B2:G2) – A simple selection that sums the values of a row.
  =SUM(A2:A8) – A simple selection that sums the values of a column.
  =SUM(A2:A7, A9, A12:A15) – A sophisticated collection that sums values from range A2 to A7, skips A8, adds A9, jumps A10 and A11, then finally adds from A12 to A15.
  =SUM(A2:A8)/20 – Shows you can also turn your function into a formula.

SUM | =SUM(B2:B11)

	A	B	C
1	**Country**	**Population**	
2	China	1,389,618,778	
3	India	1,311,559,204	
4	USA	331,883,986	
5	Indonesia	264,935,824	
6	Pakistan	210,797,836	
7	Brazil	210,301,591	
8	Nigeria	208,679,114	
9	Bangladesh	161,062,905	
10	Russia	141,944,641	
11	Mexico	127,318,112	
12	**Total**	=SUM(B2:B11)	Output = 4,358,101,991
13			
14			

2. AVERAGE

- The AVERAGE function should remind you of simple averages of data such as the average number of shareholders in a given shareholding pool.
  =AVERAGE(number1, [number2], ...)
  Example:
  =AVERAGE(B2:B11) – Shows a simple average, also similar to (SUM(B2:B11)/10)

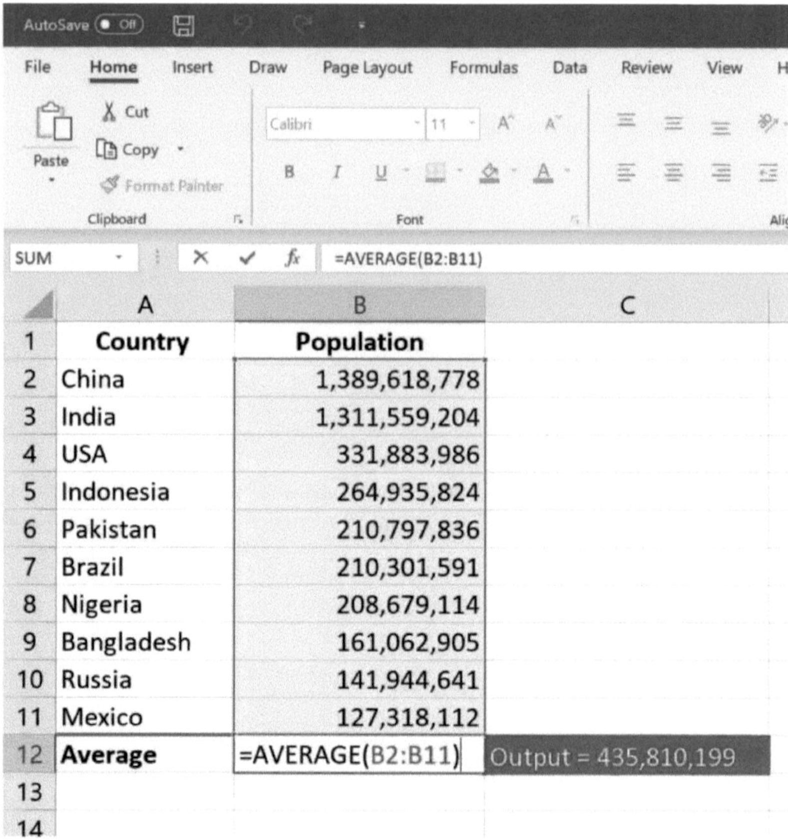

3. COUNT

- The COUNT function counts all cells in a given range that contain only numeric values.
  =COUNT(value1, [value2], ...)
  Example:
  COUNT(A:A) – Counts all values that are numerical in A column. However, you must adjust the range inside the formula to count rows.

COUNT(A1:C1) – Now it can count rows.

=COUNT(B2:B13)

	A	B	C
1	**Country**	**Population**	
2	China	1,389,618,778	
3	India	1,311,559,204	
4	USA	331,883,986	
5	Indonesia	264,935,824	
6	Pakistan	210,797,836	
7		**Empty**	Skips non-numerical values
8	Brazil	210,301,591	
9	Nigeria	208,679,114	
10			Skips empty cells
11	Bangladesh	161,062,905	
12	Russia	141,944,641	
13	Mexico	127,318,112	
14	**COUNT**	=COUNT(B2:B13)	Output = 10

4. COUNTA

- Like the COUNT function, COUNTA counts all cells in a given rage. However, it counts all cells regardless of type. That is, unlike COUNT that only counts numerics, it also counts dates, times, strings, logical values, errors, empty string, or text.
  =COUNTA(value1, [value2], ...)
  Example:
  COUNTA(C2:C13) – Counts rows 2 to 13 in column C

regardless of type. However, like COUNT, you can't use the same formula to count rows. You must make an adjustment to the selection inside the brackets – for example, COUNTA(C2:H2) will count columns C to H

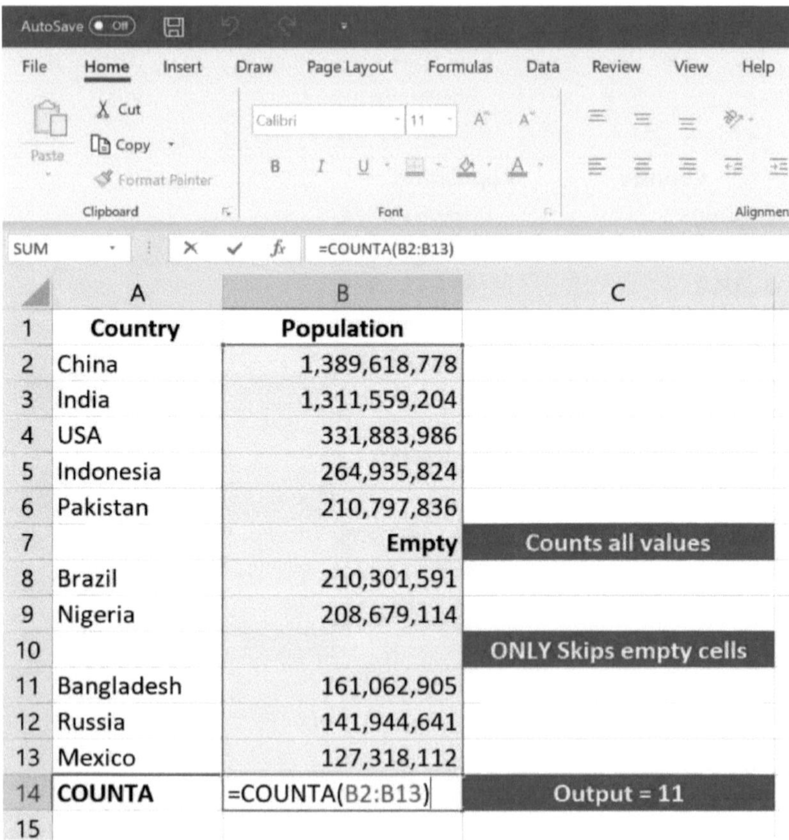

	A	B	C
1	Country	Population	
2	China	1,389,618,778	
3	India	1,311,559,204	
4	USA	331,883,986	
5	Indonesia	264,935,824	
6	Pakistan	210,797,836	
7		Empty	Counts all values
8	Brazil	210,301,591	
9	Nigeria	208,679,114	
10			ONLY Skips empty cells
11	Bangladesh	161,062,905	
12	Russia	141,944,641	
13	Mexico	127,318,112	
14	COUNTA	=COUNTA(B2:B13)	Output = 11
15			

5. IF

- The IF function is often used when you want to sort your data according to a given logic. The best part of the IF formula is that you can embed formulas and function in it.

=IF(logical_test, [value_if_true], [value_if_false])
Example:
=IF(C2<D3, ‘TRUE,’ ‘FALSE’) – Checks if the value at C3 is less than the value at D3. If the logic is true, let the cell value be TRUE, else, FALSE
=IF(SUM(C1:C10) > SUM(D1:D10), SUM(C1:C10), SUM(D1:D10)) – An example of a complex IF logic. First, it sums C1 to C10 and D1 to D10, then it compares the sum. If the sum of C1 to C10 is greater than the sum of D1 to D10, then it makes the value of a cell equal to the sum of C1 to C10. Otherwise, it makes it the SUM of C1 to C10.

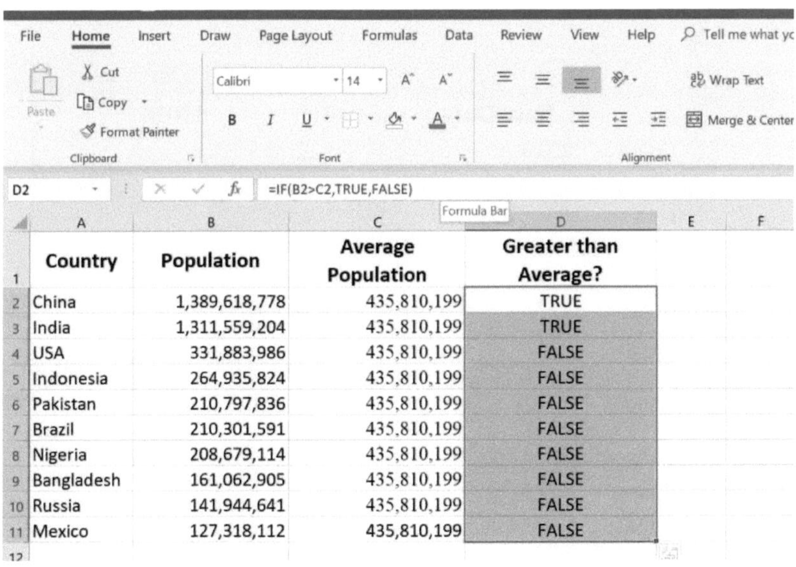

	A	B	C	D
1	Country	Population	Average Population	Greater than Average?
2	China	1,389,618,778	435,810,199	TRUE
3	India	1,311,559,204	435,810,199	TRUE
4	USA	331,883,986	435,810,199	FALSE
5	Indonesia	264,935,824	435,810,199	FALSE
6	Pakistan	210,797,836	435,810,199	FALSE
7	Brazil	210,301,591	435,810,199	FALSE
8	Nigeria	208,679,114	435,810,199	FALSE
9	Bangladesh	161,062,905	435,810,199	FALSE
10	Russia	141,944,641	435,810,199	FALSE
11	Mexico	127,318,112	435,810,199	FALSE

6. TRIM

- The TRIM function makes sure your functions do not return errors due to unruly spaces. It ensures that all empty spaces are eliminated. Unlike other functions that can operate on a range of cells, TRIM only operates on a single cell. Therefore, it comes with the downside of adding duplicated data in your spreadsheet.

=TRIM(text)

Example:

TRIM(A2) – Removes empty spaces in the value in cell A2.

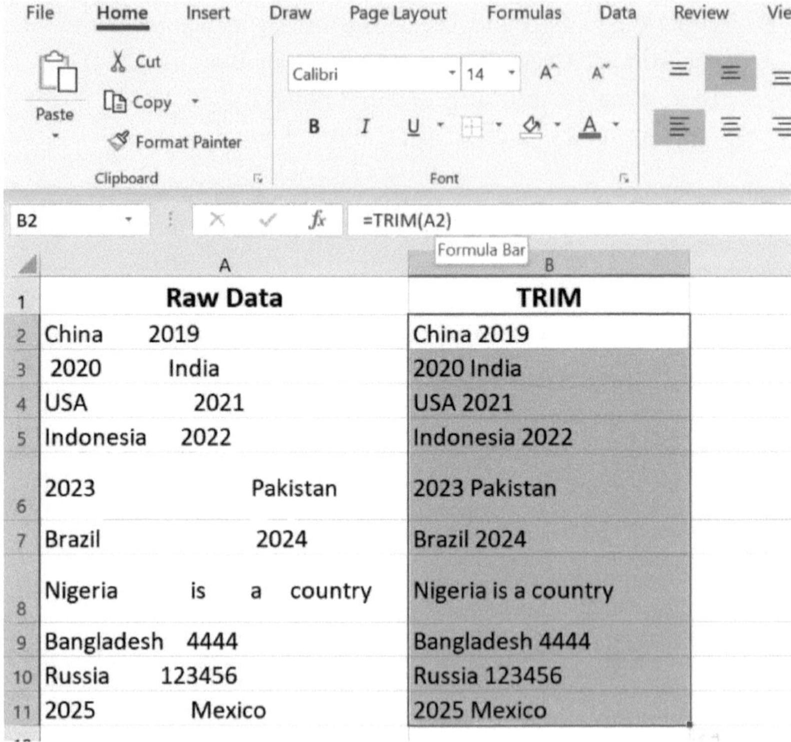

7. MAX & MIN

- The MAX and MIN functions help in finding the maximum number and the minimum number in a range of values.
  =MIN(number1, [number2], ...)

Example:
=MIN(B2:C11) – Finds the minimum number between column B from B2 and column C from C2 to row 11 in both columns B and C.

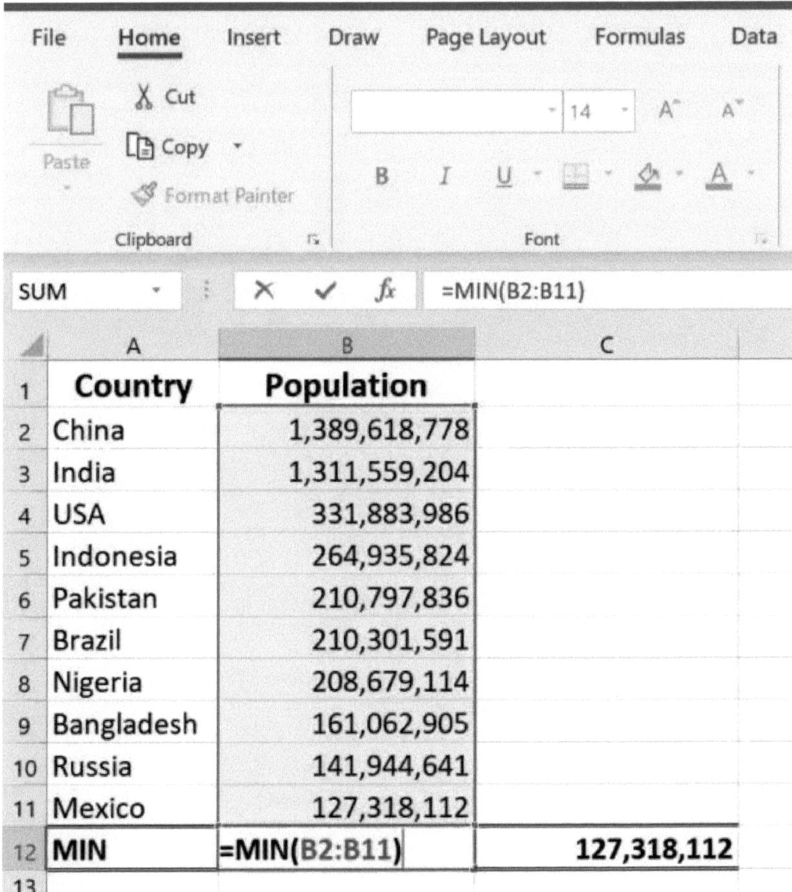

- **=MAX(number1, [number2], ...)**
  Example:

=MAX(B2:C11) – Similarly, it finds the maximum number between column B from B2 and column C from C2 to row 11 in both columns B and C.

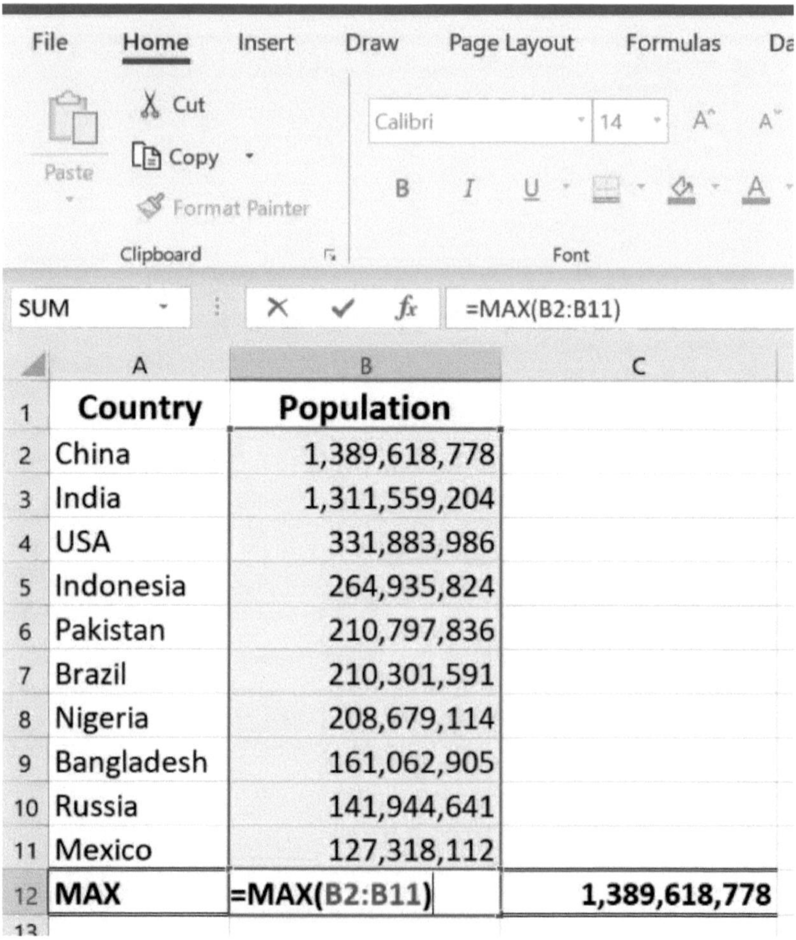
File
Home
Insert
Draw
Page Layout
Formulas
Cut
Copy
Paste
Format Painter
Clipboard
Calibri
14
Font
SUM
=MAX(B2:B11)
A
B
C
1 Country Population
2 China 1,389,618,778
3 India 1,311,559,204
4 USA 331,883,986
5 Indonesia 264,935,824
6 Pakistan 210,797,836
7 Brazil 210,301,591
8 Nigeria 208,679,114
9 Bangladesh 161,062,905
10 Russia 141,944,641
11 Mexico 127,318,112
12 MAX =MAX(B2:B11) 1,389,618,778

8. SUBTOTAL

- Moving ahead, let's now understand how the subtotal function works. The SUBTOTAL() function returns the subtotal in a database. Depending on what you want, you can select either average, count, sum, min, max, min, and others. Let's have a look at two such examples.

C5 =SUBTOTAL(1,A2:A4)

	A	B	C	D	E
1	Qty	Price per Unit	Total Sales		
2	10	30	300		
3	11	35	385		
4	12	40	480		
5		Subtotal	11		

- In the example above, we have performed the subtotal calculation on cells ranging from A2 to A4. As you can see, the function used is "=SUBTOTAL(1, A2: A4), in the subtotal list "1" refers to average. Hence, the above function will give the average of A2: A4 and the answer to it is 11, which is stored in C5.
- Similarly, "=SUBTOTAL(4, A2: A4)" selects the cell with the maximum value from A2 to A4, which is 12. Incorporating "4" in the function provides the maximum result.

C5 =SUBTOTAL(4,A2:A4)

	A	B	C	D	E
1	Qty	Price per Unit	Total Sales		
2	10	30	300		
3	11	35	385		
4	12	40	480		
5		Subtotal	12		

9. MODULUS

- The MOD() function works on returning the remainder when a particular number is divided by a divisor. Let's now have a look at the examples below for better understanding.
  In the first example, we have divided 10 by 3. The remainder is calculated using the function "=MOD(A2,3)". The result is stored in B2. We can also directly type "=MOD(10,3)" as it will give the same answer.

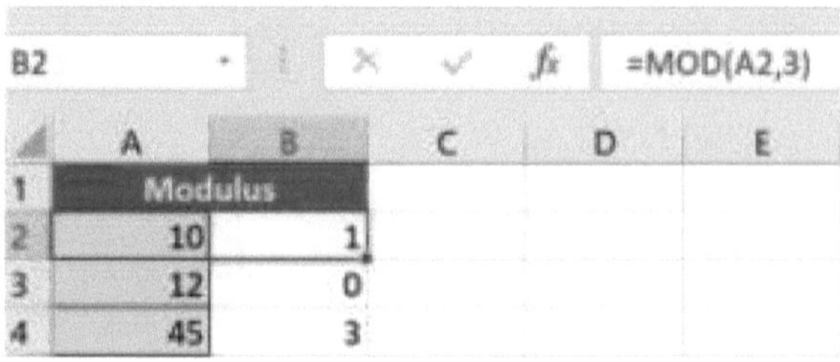

B2 =MOD(A2,3)

	A	B	C	D	E
1	Modulus				
2	10	1			
3	12	0			
4	45	3			

- Similarly, here, we have divided 12 by 4. The remainder is 0 is, which is stored in B3.

B3 =MOD(A3,4)

	A	B	C	D	E
1	Modulus				
2	10	1			
3	12	0			
4	45	3			

10. POWER

- The function "Power()" returns the result of a number raised to a certain power. Let's have a look at the examples shown below:

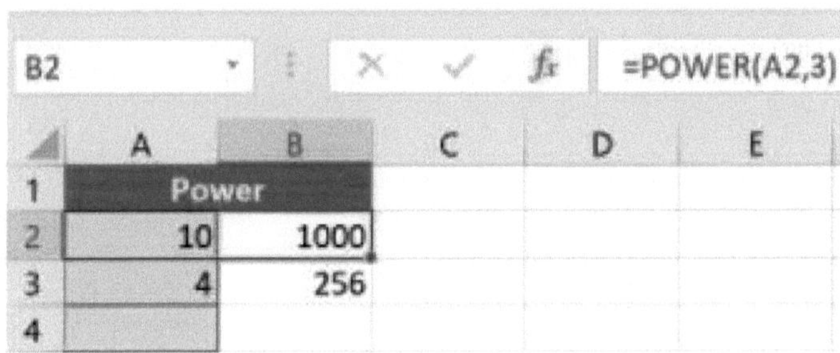

B2 =POWER(A2,3)

	A	B	C	D	E
1	Power				
2	10	1000			
3	4	256			
4					

- As you can see above, to find the power of 10 stored in A2 raised to 3, we have to type "= POWER (A2,3)". This is how power function works in Excel.

11. CEILING

- Next, we have the ceiling function. The CEILING() function rounds a number up to its nearest multiple of significance.

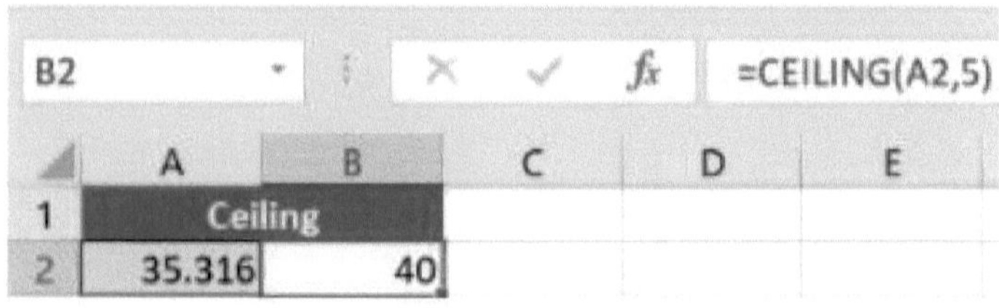

- The nearest highest multiple of 5 for 35.316 is 40.

12. FLOOR

- Contrary to the Ceiling function, the floor function rounds a number down to the nearest multiple of significance.

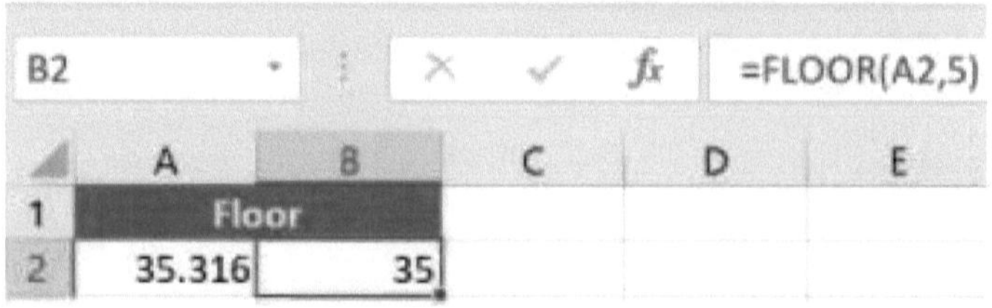

The nearest lowest multiple of 5 for 35.316 is 35.

13. CONCATENATE

- This function merges or joins several text strings into one text string. Given below are the different ways to perform this function.

- In this example, we have operated with the syntax =CONCATENATE(A25, " ", B25)

Enter Caption

- In this example, we have operated with the syntax =CONCATENATE(A27&" "&B27)

- Those were the two ways to implement the concatenation operation in Excel.

14. LEN

- The function LEN() returns the total number of characters in a string. So, it will count the overall characters, including spaces and special characters. Given below is an example of the Len function.

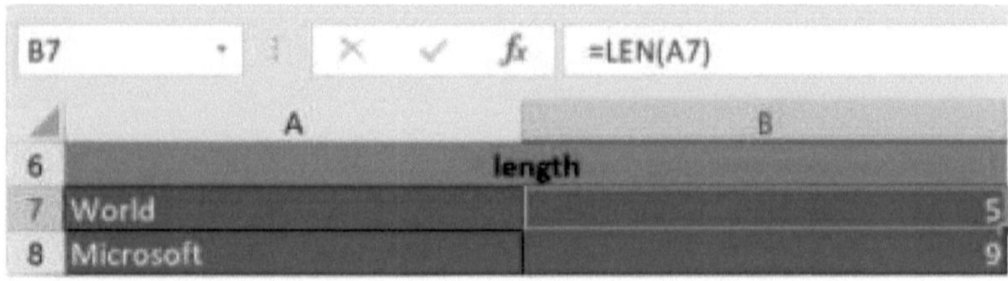

Let's now move onto the next Excel function on our list of this article.

15. REPLACE

- As the name suggests, the REPLACE() function works on replacing the part of a text string with a different text string.
- The syntax is "=REPLACE(old_text, start_num, num_chars, new_text)". Here, start_num refers to the index position you want to start replacing the characters with. Next, num_chars indicate the number of characters you want to replace.
  Let's have a look at the ways we can use this function.
- Here, we are replacing A101 with B101 by typing "=REPLACE(A15,1,1,"B")".

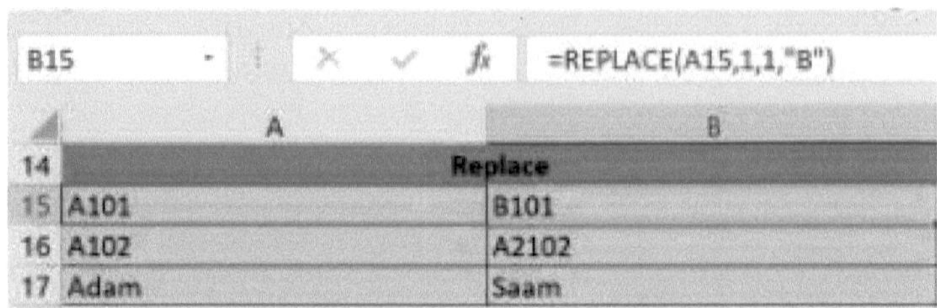

- Next, we are replacing A102 with A2102 by typing "=REPLACE(A16,1,1, "A2")".

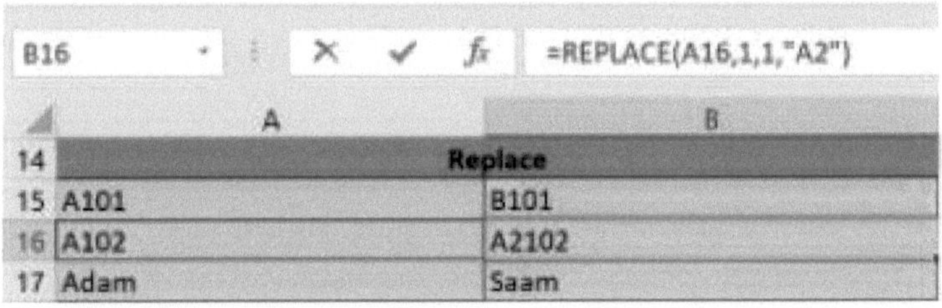

B16 =REPLACE(A16,1,1,"A2")

	A	B
14	Replace	
15	A101	B101
16	A102	A2102
17	Adam	Saam

- Finally, we are replacing Adam with Saam by typing "=REPLACE(A17,1,2, "Sa")".

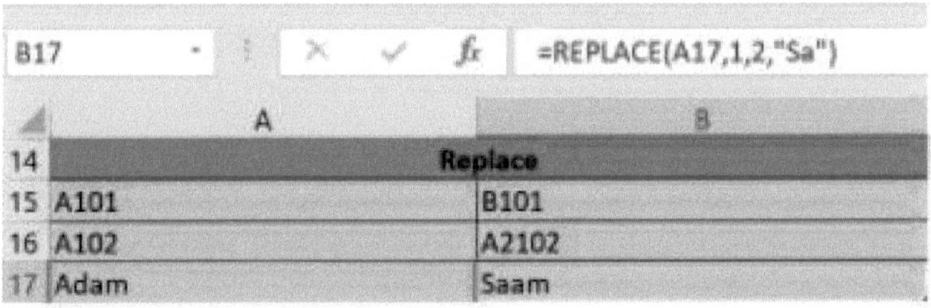

B17 =REPLACE(A17,1,2,"Sa")

	A	B
14	Replace	
15	A101	B101
16	A102	A2102
17	Adam	Saam

16. SUBSTITUTE

- The SUBSTITUTE() function replaces the existing text with a new text in a text string.

- The syntax is "=SUBSTITUTE(text, old_text, new_text, [instance_num])".
  Here, [instance_num] refers to the index position of the present texts more than once.
  Given below are a few examples of this function:
  Here, we are substituting "I like" with "He likes" by typing "=SUBSTITUTE(A20, "I like","He likes")".

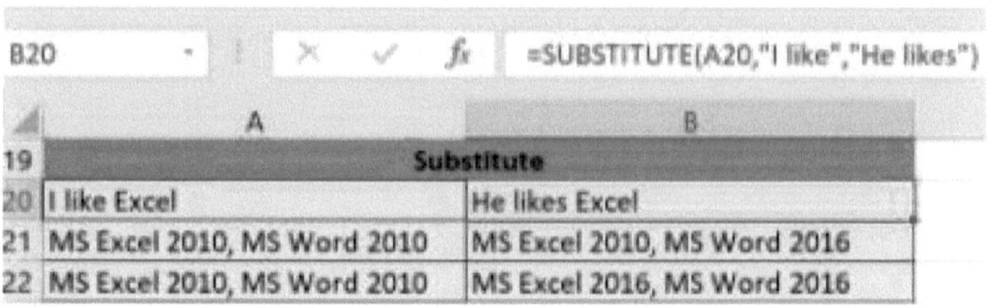

B20 =SUBSTITUTE(A20,"I like","He likes")

	A	B
19	Substitute	
20	I like Excel	He likes Excel
21	MS Excel 2010, MS Word 2010	MS Excel 2010, MS Word 2016
22	MS Excel 2010, MS Word 2010	MS Excel 2016, MS Word 2016

- Next, we are substituting the second 2010 that occurs in the original text in cell A21 with 2016 by typing "=SUBSTITUTE(A21,2010, 2016,2)".

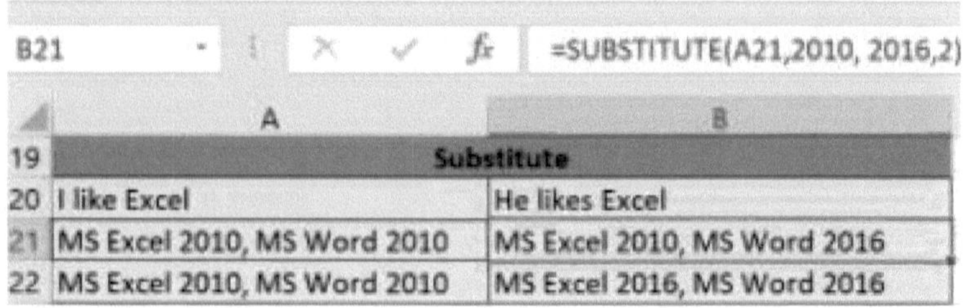

B21 =SUBSTITUTE(A21,2010, 2016,2)

	A	B
19	Substitute	
20	I like Excel	He likes Excel
21	MS Excel 2010, MS Word 2010	MS Excel 2010, MS Word 2016
22	MS Excel 2010, MS Word 2010	MS Excel 2016, MS Word 2016

- Now, we are replacing both the 2010s in the original text with 2016 by typing "=SUBSTITUTE(A22,2010,2016)".

B22 | =SUBSTITUTE(A22,2010,2016)

	A	B
19	Substitute	
20	I like Excel	He likes Excel
21	MS Excel 2010, MS Word 2010	MS Excel 2010, MS Word 2016
22	MS Excel 2010, MS Word 2010	MS Excel 2016, MS Word 2016

17. LEFT, RIGHT, MID

- The LEFT() function gives the number of characters from the start of a text string. Meanwhile, the MID() function returns the characters from the middle of a text string, given a starting position and length. Finally, the right() function returns the number of characters from the end of a text string.
  Let's understand these functions with a few examples.
  In the example below, we use the function left to obtain the leftmost word on the sentence in cell A5.

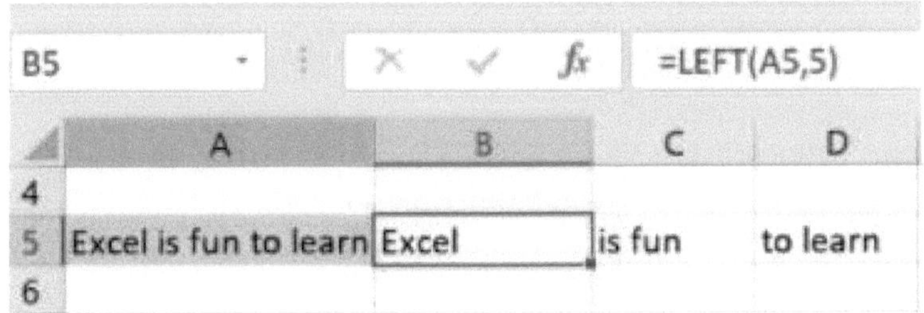

B5 | =LEFT(A5,5)

	A	B	C	D
4				
5	Excel is fun to learn	Excel	is fun	to learn
6				

- Shown below is an example using the mid function.

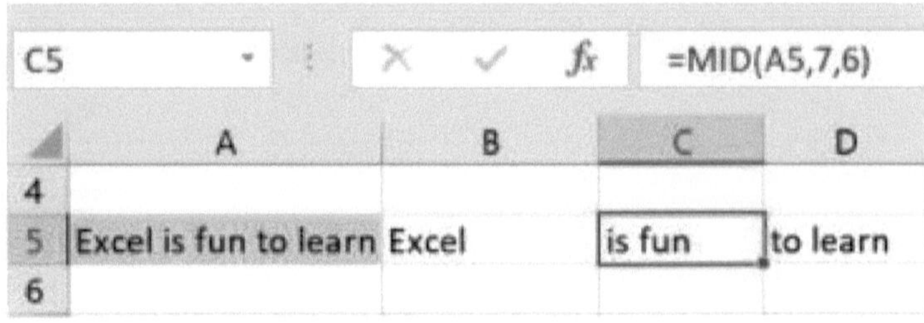

- Here, we have an example of the right function.

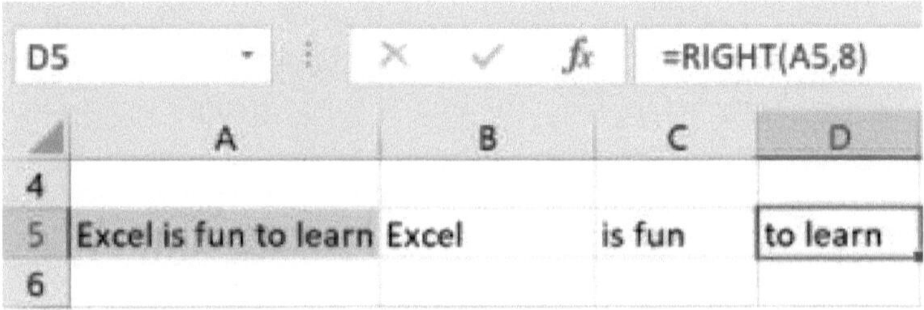

18. UPPER, LOWER, PROPER

- The UPPER() function converts any text string to uppercase. In contrast, the LOWER() function converts any text string to lowercase. The PROPER() function converts any text string to proper case, i.e., the first letter in each word will be in uppercase, and all the other will be in lowercase.
  Let's understand this better with the following examples:

- Here, we have converted the text in A6 to a full uppercase one in A7.

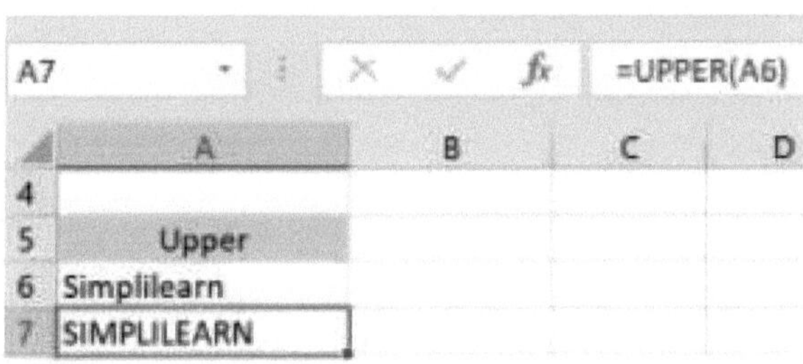

- Now, we have converted the text in A6 to a full lowercase one, as seen in A7.

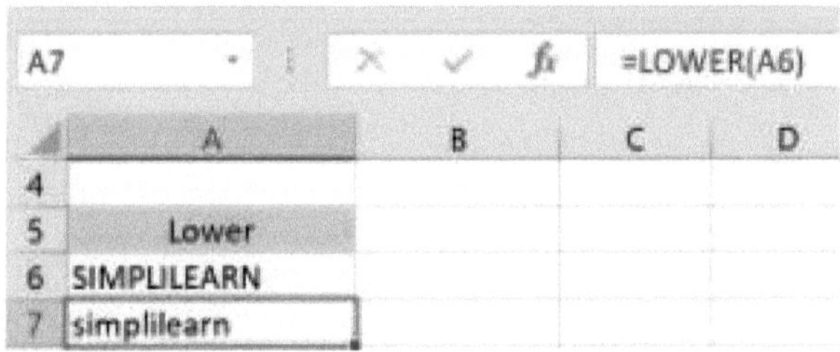

- Finally, we have converted the improper text in A6 to a clean and proper format in A7.

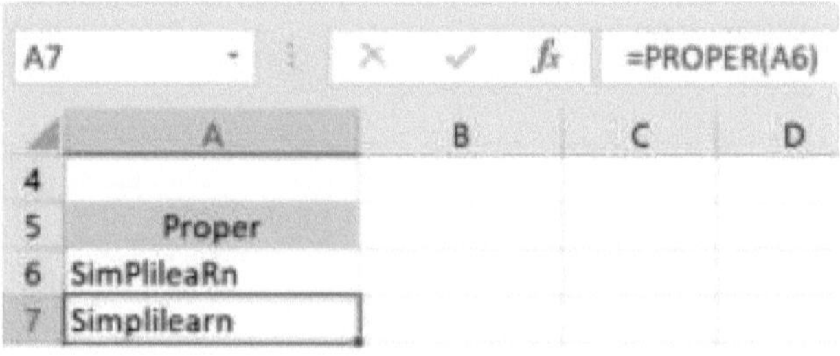

19. NOW()

- The NOW() function in Excel gives the current system date and time.

- The result of the NOW() function will change based on your system date and time.

20. TODAY()

- The TODAY() function in Excel provides the current system date.
- The function DAY() is used to return the day of the month. It will be a number between 1 to 31. 1 is the first day of the month, 31 is the last day of the month.

- The MONTH() function returns the month, a number from 1 to 12, where 1 is January and 12 is December.
- The YEAR() function, as the name suggests, returns the year from a date value.

21. TIME()

- The TIME() function converts hours, minutes, seconds given as numbers to an Excel serial number, formatted with a time format.

22. HOUR, MINUTE, SECOND

- The HOUR() function generates the hour from a time value as a number from 0 to 23. Here, 0 means 12 AM and 23 is 11 PM.
- The function MINUTE(), returns the minute from a time value as a number from 0 to 59.
- The SECOND() function returns the second from a time value as a number from 0 to 59.

23. DATEDIF

- The DATEDIF() function provides the difference between two dates in terms of years, months, or days.
- Below is an example of a DATEDIF function where we calculate the current age of a person based on two given dates, the date of birth and today's date.

Calculate Age	Datedif
DOB	30-12-1994
Today	24-08-2020
Age	=DATEDIF(B12,B13,"y")

➡

Calculate Age	Datedif
DOB	30-12-1994
Today	24-08-2020
Age	25

- Now, let's skin through a few critical advanced functions in Excel that are popularly used to analyze data and create reports.

24. VLOOKUP

- Next up in this article is the VLOOKUP() function. This stands for the vertical lookup that is responsible for looking for a particular value in the leftmost column of a table. It then returns a value in the same row from a column you specify.
- Below are the arguments for the VLOOKUP function:
- lookup_value - This is the value that you have to look for in the first column of a table.
- table - This indicates the table from which the value is retrieved.
- col_index - The column in the table from the value is to be retrieved.
- range_lookup - [optional] TRUE = approximate match (default). FALSE = exact match.
- We will use the below table to learn how the VLOOKUP function works.
- If you wanted to find the department to which Stuart belongs, you could use the VLOOKUP function as shown below:

	A	B	C	D	E
1	First Name	Last Name	Department	City	Date Hired
2	Ben	Zampa	HR	Chicago	10-11-2001
3	Stuart	Carry	Marketing	Kansas	20-06-2002
4	Jenson	Button	Operations	New York	01-12-2004
5	Lucy	Davis	Sales	Los Angeles	25-02-2011
6	Trent	Patinson	IT	Boston	17-08-2015
7	Jhonny	Evans	Sales	Houston	10-01-2018

- Here, A11 cell has the lookup value, A2: E7 is the table array, 3 is the column index number with information about departments, and 0 is the range lookup.

9	Vlookup				
10	First Name	Last Name	Department	City	Date Hired
11	Stuart		=VLOOKUP(A11,A2:E7,3,0)		

- If you hit enter, it will return "Marketing", indicating that Stuart is from the marketing department.

9	Vlookup				
10	First Name	Last Name	Department	City	Date Hired
11	Stuart		Marketing		

25. HLOOKUP

- Similar to VLOOKUP, we have another function called HLOOKUP() or horizontal lookup. The function HLOOKUP looks for a value in the top row of a table or array of benefits. It gives the value in the same column from a row you specify.
  Below are the arguments for the HLOOKUP function:
- lookup_value - This indicates the value to lookup.
- table - This is the table from which you have to retrieve data.
- row_index - This is the row number from which to retrieve data.
- range_lookup - [optional] This is a boolean to indicate an exact match or approximate match.

- The default value is TRUE, meaning an approximate match. Given the below table, let's see how you can find the city of Jenson using HLOOKUP.

G	H	I	J	K	L	M
First Name	Ben	Stuart	Jenson	Lucy	Trent	Jhonny
Last Name	Zampa	Carry	Button	Davis	Patinson	Evans
Department	HR	Marketing	Operations	Sales	IT	Sales
City	Chicago	Kansas	New York	Los Angeles	Boston	Houston
Date Hired	10-11-2001	20-06-2002	01-12-2004	25-02-2011	17-08-2015	10-01-2018

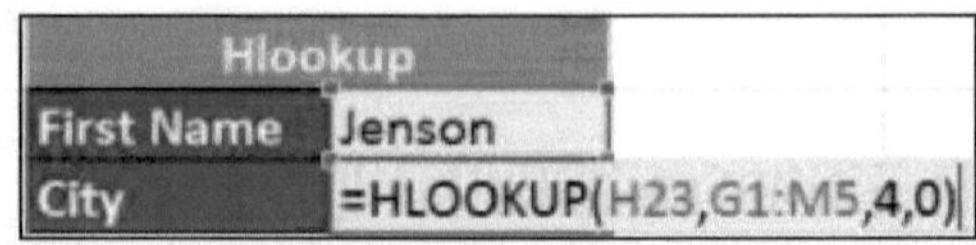

Hlookup	
First Name	Jenson
City	=HLOOKUP(H23,G1:M5,4,0)

Here, H23 has the lookup value, i.e., Jenson, G1:M5 is the table array, 4 is the row index number, 0 is for an approximate match. Once you hit enter, it will return "New York".

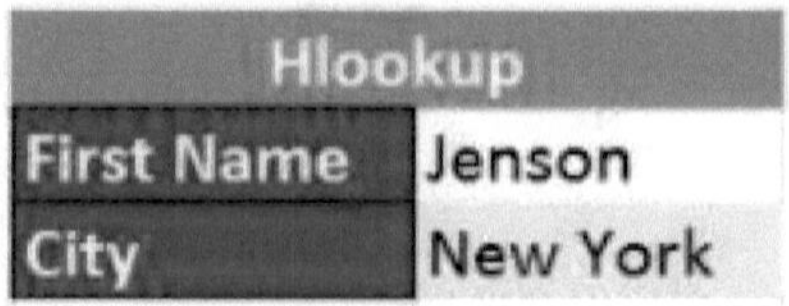

Hlookup	
First Name	Jenson
City	New York

26. INDEX-MATCH

- The INDEX-MATCH function is used to return a value in a column to the left. With VLOOKUP, you're stuck returning an appraisal from a column to the right. Another reason to use index-match instead of VLOOKUP is that VLOOKUP needs more processing power from Excel. This is because it needs to evaluate the entire table array which you've selected. With

INDEX-MATCH, Excel only has to consider the lookup column and the return column.

Using the below table, let's see how you can find the city where Jenson resides.

Z	AA	AB	AC	AD
First Name	Last Name	Department	City	Date Hired
Ben	Button	HR	Chicago	10-11-2001
Jenson	Carry	IT	Kansas	20-06-2002
Jhonny	Davis	Marketing	New York	01-12-2004
Lucy	Evans	Operations	Los Angeles	25-02-2011
Stuart	Patinson	Sales	Boston	17-08-2015
Trent	Zampa	Sales	Houston	10-01-2018

Index Match	
First Name	City
Jenson	=INDEX(AC1:AC7,MATCH(AB12,Z1:Z7,0))

Index Match	
First Name	City
Jenson	Kansas

Now, let's find the department of Zampa.

Last Name	City	Department
Zampa	Houston	[illegible]

Last Name	City	Department
Zampa	Houston	Sales

27. COUNTIF

The function COUNTIF() is used to count the total number of cells within a range that meet the given condition.

Below is a coronavirus sample dataset with information regarding the coronavirus cases and deaths in each country and region.

Let's find the number of times Afghanistan is present in the table.

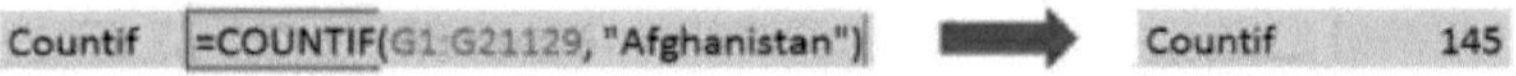

The COUNTIFS function counts the number of cells specified by a given set of conditions.

If you want to count the number of days in which the cases in India have been greater than 100. Here is how you can use the COUNTIFS function.

28. SUMIF

The SUMIF() function adds the cells specified by a given condition or criteria.

Below is the coronavirus dataset using which we will find the total number of cases in India till 3rd Jun 2020. (Our dataset has information from 31st Dec 2020 to 3rd Jun 2020).

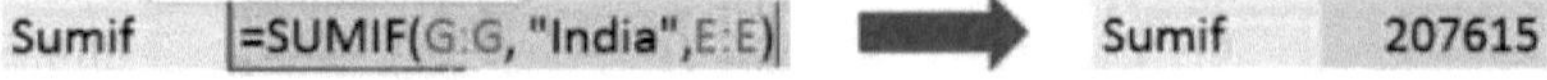

The SUMIFS() function adds the cells specified by a given set of conditions or criteria.

Let's find the total cases in France on those days when the deaths have been less than 100.

Gain expertise in the latest Business analytics tools and techniques with the Business Analyst Master's Program. Enroll now!

Conclusion

Excel is a really powerful spreadsheet application for data analysis and reporting. After reading this article, you would have learned the important Excel formulas and functions that will help you perform your tasks better and faster. We looked at numeric, text, data-time, and advanced Excel formulas and functions. Needless to say, Excel knowledge goes a long way in shaping many careers.

Do you have any questions related to this article on Excel Formulas? If yes, then please let us know in the comments section of the article. Our team of experts will help you solve your queries right away.

To kick-start your fruitful career in Excel, please click on the following link: Business Analytics with Excel.

CHAPTER FOUR

Advance Formulas

Compatibility Excel Formulas & Functions

1. **CONCATENATE**
   =CONCATENATE(text1,text2,...)
   Joins several text items into one text item. Easier to use '&' instead of the function usually.
2. **FLOOR**
   =FLOOR(number,significance)
   Rounds a number down, toward zero
3. **BINOMDIST**
   =BINOMDIST(number_s,trials,probability_s,cumulative)
   Returns the individual term binomial distribution probability
4. **CHIDIST**
   =CHIDIST(x,deg_freedom)
   Returns the one-tailed probability of the chi-squared distribution
5. **CHIINV**
   =CHITEST(actual_range,expected_range)
   Returns the test for independence
6. **CONFIDENCE**
   =CONFIDENCE(alpha,standard_dev,size)
   Returns the confidence interval for a population mean
7. **FTEST**
   =FTEST(array1,array2)

8. **LOGINV**
   =LOGINV(probability,mean,standard_dev)
   Returns the inverse of the lognormal cumulative distribution
9. **LOGNORMDIST**
   =LOGNORMDIST(x,mean,standard_dev)
   Returns the cumulative lognormal distribution
10. **MODE**
    =MODE(number1,number2,...)
    Returns the most common value in a data set
11. **NORMDIST**
    =NORMDIST(x,mean,standard_dev,cumulative)
    Returns the normal cumulative distribution
12. **NORMINV**
    =NORMINV(probability,mean,standard_dev)
    Returns the inverse of the normal cumulative distribution
13. **NORMSDIST**
    =NORMSDIST(z)
    Returns the standard normal cumulative distribution
14. **NORMSINV**
    =NORMSINV(probability)
    Returns the inverse of the standard normal cumulative distribution
15. **PERCENTILE**
    =PERCENTILE(array,k)
    Returns the k-th percentile of values in a range
16. **PERCENTRANK**
    =PERCENTRANK(array,x,significance)
    Returns the percentage rank of a value in a data set
17. **POISSON**
    =POISSON(x,mean,cumulative)
    Returns the Poisson distribution
18. **QUARTILE**
    =QUARTILE(array,quart)
    Returns the quartile of a data set

19. **RANK**
    =RANK(number,ref,order)
    Returns the rank of a number in a list of numbers
20. **STDEV**
    =STDEV(number1,number2,...)
    Estimates standard deviation based on a sample
21. **STDEVP**
    =STDEVP(number1,number2,...)
    Calculates standard deviation based on the entire population
22. **TDIST**
    =TDIST(x,deg_freedom,tails)
    Returns the Student's t-distribution
23. **TINV**
    =TINV(probability,deg_freedom)
    Returns the inverse of the Student's t-distribution
24. **VAR**
    =VAR(number1,number2,...)
    Estimates variance based on a sample
25. **VARP**
    =VARP(number1,number2,...)
    Calculates variance based on the entire population
26. **FINV**
    =FINV(probability,deg_freedom1,deg_freedom2)
    Returns the inverse of the F probability distribution
27. **FORECAST**
    =FORECAST(x,known_y's,known_x's)
    Returns a value along a linear trend
28. **BETADIST**
    =BETADIST(x,alpha,beta,A,B)
    Returns the beta cumulative distribution function
29. **BETAINV**
    =BETAINV(probability,alpha,beta,A,B)
    Returns the inverse of the cumulative distribution function for a specified beta distribution

30. **COVAR**
=COVAR(array1,array2)
Returns covariance, the average of the products of paired deviations
31. **CRITBINOM**
=CRITBINOM(trials,probability_s,alpha)
Returns the smallest value for which the cumulative binomial distribution is less than or equal to a criterion value
32. **EXPONDIST**
=EXPONDIST(x,lambda,cumulative)
Returns the exponential distribution
33. **POISSON**
=POISSON(x,mean,cumulative)
Returns the Poisson distribution
34. **FDIST**
=FDIST(x,deg_freedom1,deg_freedom2)
Returns the F probability distribution
35. **GAMMADIST**
=GAMMADIST(x,alpha,beta,cumulative)
Returns the gamma distribution
36. **GAMMAINV**
=GAMMAINV(probability,alpha,beta)
Returns the inverse of the gamma cumulative distribution
37. **HYPGEOMDIST**
=HYPGEOMDIST(sample_s,number_sample,population_s,number_po
Returns the hypergeometric distribution
38. **NEGBINOMDIST**
=NEGBINOMDIST(number_f,number_s,probability_s)
Returns the negative binomial distribution
39. **TTEST**
=TTEST(array1,array2,tails,type)
Returns the probability associated with a Student's t-test
40. **WEIBULL**
=WEIBULL(x,alpha,beta,cumulative)
Calculates variance based on the entire population, including

numbers, text, and logical values

41. **ZTEST**
=ZTEST(array,x,sigma)
Returns the one-tailed probability-value of a z-test

Cube Excel Formulas & Functions

1. **CUBEKPIMEMBER**
=CUBEKPIMEMBER(connection,kpi_name,kpi_property,caption)
Returns a key performance indicator (KPI) name, property, and measure, and displays the name and property in the cell. A KPI is a quantifiable measurement, such as monthly gross profit or quarterly employee turnover, used to monitor an organization's performance.
2. **CUBEMEMBER**
=CUBEMEMBER(connection,member_expression,caption)
Returns a member or tuple in a cube hierarchy. Use to validate that the member or tuple exists in the cube.
3. **CUBEMEMBERPROPERTY**
=CUBEMEMBERPROPERTY(connection,member_expression,proper
Returns the value of a member property in the cube. Use to validate that a member name exists within the cube and to return the specified property for this member.
4. **CUBERANKEDMEMBER**
=CUBERANKEDMEMBER(connection,set_expression,rank,caption)
Returns the nth, or ranked, member in a set. Use to return one or more elements in a set, such as the top sales performer or top 10 students.
5. **CUBESET**
=CUBESET(connection,set_expression,caption,sort_order,sort_by)
Defines a calculated set of members or tuples by sending a set expression to the cube on the server, which creates the set, and then returns that set to Microsoft Office Excel.

6. **CUBESETCOUNT**
   =CUBESETCOUNT(set)
   Returns the number of items in a set.
7. **CUBEVALUE**
   =CUBEVALUE(connection,member_expression1,...)
   Returns an aggregated value from a cube

Database Excel Formulas & Functions

1. **DGET**
   =DGET(database,field,criteria)
   Extracts from a database a single record that matches the specified criteria
2. **DSUM**
   =DSUM(database,field,criteria)
   Adds the numbers in the field column of records in the database that match the criteria
3. **DAVERAGE**
   =DAVERAGE(database,field,criteria)
   Returns the average of selected database entries
4. **DCOUNT**
   =DCOUNT(database,field,criteria)
   Counts the cells that contain numbers in a database
5. **DCOUNTA**
   =DCOUNTA(database,field,criteria)
   Counts nonblank cells in a database
6. **DMAX**
   =DMAX(database,field,criteria)
   Returns the maximum value from selected database entries
7. **DMIN**
   =DMIN(database,field,criteria)
   Returns the minimum value from selected database entries
8. **DPRODUCT**
   =DPRODUCT(database,field,criteria)
   Multiplies the values in a particular field of records that match

the criteria in a database

9. **DSTDEV**
   =DSTDEV(database,field,criteria)
   Estimates the standard deviation based on a sample of selected database entries
10. **DSTDEVP**
    =DSTDEVP(database,field,criteria)
    Calculates the standard deviation based on the entire population of selected database entries
11. **DVAR**
    =DVAR(database,field,criteria)
    Estimates variance based on a sample from selected database entries
12. **DVARP**
    =DVARP(database,field,criteria)
    Calculates variance based on the entire population of selected database entries

Date & Time Excel Formulas & Functions

1. **DATE**
   =DATE(year,month,day)
   Returns the serial number of a particular date
2. **DATEVALUE**
   =DATEVALUE(date_text)
   Converts a date in the form of text to a serial number
3. **DAY**
   =DAY(serial_number)
   Converts a serial number to a day of the month
4. **HOUR**
   =HOUR(serial_number)
   Converts a serial number to an hour
5. **MINUTE**
   =MINUTE(serial_number)
   Converts a serial number to a minute

6. **MONTH**
   =MONTH(serial_number)
   Converts a serial number to a month
7. **NOW**
   =NOW()
   Returns the serial number of the current date and time
8. **SECOND**
   =SECOND(serial_number)
   Converts a serial number to a second
9. **TIME**
   =TIME(hour,minute,second)
   Returns the serial number of a particular time
10. **TIMEVALUE**
    =TIMEVALUE(time_text)
    Converts a time in the form of text to a serial number
11. **TODAY**
    =TODAY()
    Returns the serial number of today's date
12. **YEAR**
    =YEAR(serial_number)
    Converts a serial number to a year
13. **DAYS360**
    =DAYS360(start_date,end_date,method)
    Calculates the number of days between two dates based on a 360-day year
14. **EDATE**
    =EDATE(start_date,months)
    Returns the serial number of the date that is the indicated number of months before or after the start date
15. **EOMONTH**
    =EOMONTH(start_date,months)
    Returns the serial number of the last day of the month before or after a specified number of months
16. **NETWORKDAYS**
    =NETWORKDAYS(start_date,end_date,[holidays])

Returns the number of whole workdays between two dates

17. **NETWORKDAYS.INTL**
    =NETWORKDAYS.INTL(start_date,end_date,[weekend],[holidays])
    Returns the number of whole workdays between two dates using parameters to indicate which and how many days are weekend days
18. **WEEKDAY**
    =WEEKDAY(serial_number,[return_type])
    Converts a serial number to a day of the week
19. **WEEKNUM**
    =WEEKNUM(serial_number,[return_type])
    Converts a serial number to a number representing where the week falls numerically with a year
20. **WORKDAY**
    =WORKDAY(start_date, days, [holidays])
    Returns the serial number of the date before or after a specified number of workdays
21. **WORKDAY.INTL**
    =WORKDAY.INTL(start_date,days,weekend,holidays)
    Returns the serial number of the date before or after a specified number of workdays using parameters to indicate which and how many days are weekend days
22. **YEARFRAC**
    =YEARFRAC(start_date,end_date,basis)
    Returns the year fraction representing the number of whole days between start_date and end_date

Information Excel Formulas & Functions

1. **CELL**
   =CELL(info_type, [reference])
   Returns information about the formatting, location, or contents of a cell
2. **ISBLANK**
   =ISBLANK(value)

Returns TRUE if the value is blank

3. **ISERROR**
   =ISERROR(value)
   Returns TRUE if the value is any error value
4. **ISNONTEXT**
   =ISNONTEXT(value)
   Returns TRUE if the value is not text
5. **ISNUMBER**
   =ISNUMBER(value)
   Returns TRUE if the value is a number
6. **ISTEXT**
   =ISTEXT(value)
   Returns TRUE if the value is text
7. **ERROR.TYPE**
   =ERROR.TYPE(error_val)
   Returns a number corresponding to an error type
8. **INFO**
   =INFO(type_text)
   Returns information about the current operating environment
9. **ISERR**
   =ISERR(value)
   Returns TRUE if the value is any error value except #N/A
10. **ISEVEN**
    =ISEVEN(number)
    Returns TRUE if the number is even
11. **ISLOGICAL**
    =ISLOGICAL(value)
    Returns TRUE if the value is a logical value
12. **ISNA**
    =ISNA(value)
    Returns TRUE if the value is the #N/A error value
13. **ISODD**
    =ISODD(number)
    Returns TRUE if the number is odd

14. **ISREF**
    =ISREF(value)
    Returns TRUE if the value is a reference
15. **N**
    =N(value)
    Returns a value converted to a number
16. **NA**
    =NA()
    Returns the error value #N/A
17. **TYPE**
    =TYPE(value)
    Returns a number indicating the data type of a value

Logical Excel Formulas & Functions

1. **AND**
   =AND(logical1,logical2,...)
   Returns TRUE if all of its arguments are TRUE
2. **FALSE**
   =FALSE
   Returns the logical value FALSE
3. **IF**
   =IF(logical_test, [value_if_true], [value_if_false])
   Specifies a logical test to perform
4. **IFERROR**
   =IFERROR(value, value_if_error)
   Returns a value you specify if a formula evaluates to an error; otherwise, returns the result of the formula
5. **NOT**
   =NOT(logical)
   Reverses the logic of its argument
6. **OR**
   =OR(logical1,logical2,...)
   Returns TRUE if any argument is TRUE

7. **TRUE**
   =TRUE
   Returns the logical value TRUE
8. **LOOKUP**
   =LOOKUP(lookup_value, array)– 2 types
   Looks up values in a vector or array

Lookup & Reference Excel Formulas & Functions

1. **ADDRESS**
   =ADDRESS(row_num, column_num, [abs_num], [a1], [sheet_text])
   Returns a reference as text to a single cell in a worksheet
2. **COLUMN**
   =COLUMN([reference])
   Returns the column number of a reference
3. **COLUMNS**
   =COLUMNS(array)
   Returns the number of columns in a reference
4. **HLOOKUP**
   =HLOOKUP(lookup_value,table_array,row_index_num,[range_lookup
   Looks in the top row of an array and returns the value of the indicated cell
5. **INDEX**
   =INDEX(array,row_num,[column_num])– 2 types
   Uses an index to choose a value from a reference or array
6. **INDIRECT**
   =INDIRECT(ref_text,a1)
   Returns a reference indicated by a text value
7. **MATCH**
   =MATCH(lookup_value,lookup_array,match_type)
   Looks up values in a reference or array
8. **OFFSET**
   =OFFSET(reference,rows,cols,height,width)
   Returns a reference offset from a given reference

9. **ROW**
   =ROW([reference])
   Returns the row number of a reference
10. **ROWS**
    =ROWS(array)
    Returns the number of rows in a reference
11. **VLOOKUP**
    =VLOOKUP(lookup_value,table_array,col_index_num,[range_looku
    Looks in the first column of an array and moves across the row to return the value of a cell
12. **CHOOSE**
    =CHOOSE(index_num,value1,value2,...)
    Chooses a value from a list of values
13. **GETPIVOTDATA**
    =GETPIVOTDATA(data_field,pivot_table,field,item,...)
    Returns data stored in a PivotTable report
14. **HYPERLINK**
    =HYPERLINK(link_location,friendly_name)
    Creates a shortcut or jump that opens a document stored on a network server, an intranet, or the Internet
15. **TRANSPOSE**
    =TRANSPOSE(array)
    Returns the transpose of an array
16. **AREAS**
    =AREAS(reference)
    Returns the number of areas in a reference
17. **RTD**
    =RTD(progID,server,topic1,topic2,...)
    Retrieves real-time data from a program that supports COM automation (Automation: A way to work with an application's objects from another application or development tool. Formerly called OLE Automation, Automation is an industry-standard and a feature of the Component Object Model (COM).)

Text Excel Formulas & Functions

1. **EXACT**
   =EXACT(text1,text2)
   Checks to see if two text values are identical
2. **LOWER**
   =LOWER(text)
   Converts text to lowercase
3. **PROPER**
   =PROPER(text)
   Capitalizes the first letter in each word of a text value
4. **TRIM**
   =TRIM(text)
   Removes spaces from text
5. **UPPER**
   =UPPER(text)
   Converts text to uppercase
6. **CHAR**
   =CHAR(number)
   Returns the character specified by the code number
7. **CLEAN**
   =CLEAN(text)
   Removes all nonprintable characters from text
8. **CODE**
   =CODE(text)
   Returns a numeric code for the first character in a text string
9. **DOLLAR**
   =DOLLAR(number,decimals)
   Converts a number to text, using the $ (dollar) currency format
10. **FIXED**
    =FIXED(number,decimals,no_commas)
    Formats a number as text with a fixed number of decimals
11. **PHONETIC**
    =PHONETIC(reference)
    Extracts the phonetic (furigana) characters from a text string
12. **REPT**
    =REPT(text,number_times)

Repeats text a given number of times

13. **SUBSTITUTE**
    =SUBSTITUTE(text,old_text,new_text,instance_num)
    Substitutes new text for old text in a text string
14. **T**
    =T(value)
    Converts its arguments to text
15. **VALUE**
    =VALUE(text)
    Converts a text argument to a number
16. **ASC**
    =ASC(text)
    Changes full-width (double-byte) English letters or katakana within a character string to half-width (single-byte) characters
17. **BAHTTEXT**
    =BAHTTEXT(number)
    Converts a number to text, using the ß (baht) currency format

Most Common Excel Formulas & Functions

1. **FIND**
   =FIND(find_text,within_text,start_num)
   Finds one text value within another (case-sensitive)
2. **LEFT**
   =LEFT(text,num_chars)
   Returns the leftmost characters from a text value
3. **LEN**
   =LEN(text)
   Returns the number of characters in a text string
4. **MID**
   =MID(text,start_num,num_chars)
   Returns a specific number of characters from a text string starting at the position you specify
5. **REPLACE**
   =REPLACE(old_text,start_num,num_chars,new_text)

Replaces characters within text

6. **RIGHT**
   =RIGHT(text,num_chars)
   Returns the rightmost characters from a text value
7. **SEARCH**
   =SEARCH(find_text,within_text,start_num)
   Finds one text value within another (not case-sensitive)

Engineering Excel Formulas & Functions

1. **CONVERT**
   =CONVERT(number,from_unit,to_unit)
   Converts a number from one measurement system to another
2. **DELTA**
   =DELTA(number1,number2)
   Tests whether two values are equal
3. **ERF**
   =ERF(lower_limit,upper_limit)
   Returns the error function
4. **ERFC**
   =ERFC(x)
   Returns the complementary error function
5. **GESTEP**
   =GESTEP(number,step)
   Tests whether a number is greater than a threshold value
6. **ERF.PRECISE**
   =ERF.PRECISE(X)
   Returns the error function
7. **ERFC.PRECISE**
   =ERFC.PRECISE(X)
   Returns the complementary ERF function integrated between x and infinity
8. **BESSELI**
   =BESSELI(x,n)
   Returns the modified Bessel function In(x)

9. **BESSELJ**
   =BESSELJ(x,n)
   Returns the Bessel function Jn(x)
10. **BESSELK**
    =BESSELK(x,n)
    Returns the modified Bessel function Kn(x)
11. **BESSELY**
    =BESSELY(x,n)
    Returns the Bessel function Yn(x)
12. **BIN2DEC**
    =BIN2DEC(number)
    Converts a binary number to decimal
13. **BIN2HEX**
    =BIN2HEX(number,places)
    Converts a binary number to hexadecimal
14. **DEC2OCT**
    =DEC2OCT(number,places)
    Converts a decimal number to octal
15. **HEX2BIN**
    =HEX2BIN(number,places)
    Converts a hexadecimal number to binary
16. **HEX2DEC**
    =HEX2DEC(number)
    Converts a hexadecimal number to decimal
17. **HEX2OCT**
    =HEX2OCT(number,places)
    Converts a hexadecimal number to octal
18. **IMABS**
    =IMABS(inumber)
    Returns the absolute value (modulus) of a complex number
19. **IMAGINARY**
    =IMAGINARY(inumber)
    Returns the imaginary coefficient of a complex number
20. **IMARGUMENT**
    =IMARGUMENT(inumber)

Returns the argument theta, an angle expressed in radians

21. **IMCONJUGATE**
    =IMCONJUGATE(inumber)
    Returns the complex conjugate of a complex number
22. **IMCOS**
    =IMCOS(inumber)
    Returns the cosine of a complex number
23. **IMDIV**
    =IMDIV(inumber1,inumber2)
    Returns the quotient of two complex numbers
24. **IMEXP**
    =IMEXP(inumber)
    Returns the exponential of a complex number
25. **IMLN**
    =IMLN(inumber)
    Returns the natural logarithm of a complex number
26. **IMLOG10**
    =IMLOG10(inumber)
    Returns the base-10 logarithm of a complex number
27. **IMLOG2**
    =IMLOG2(inumber)
    Returns the base-2 logarithm of a complex number
28. **IMPOWER**
    =IMPOWER(inumber,number)
    Returns a complex number raised to an integer power
29. **IMPRODUCT**
    =IMPRODUCT(inumber1,inumber2,...)
    Returns the product of complex numbers
30. **IMREAL**
    =IMREAL(inumber)
    Returns the real coefficient of a complex number
31. **IMSIN**
    =IMSIN(inumber)
    Returns the sine of a complex number

32. **IMSQRT**
    =IMSQRT(inumber)
    Returns the square root of a complex number
33. **IMSUB**
    =IMSUB(inumber1,inumber2)
    Returns the difference between two complex numbers
34. **IMSUM**
    =IMSUM(inumber1,inumber2,...)
    Returns the sum of complex numbers
35. **OCT2BIN**
    =OCT2BIN(number,places)
    Converts an octal number to binary
36. **OCT2DEC**
    =OCT2DEC(number)
    Converts an octal number to decimal
37. **OCT2HEX**
    =OCT2HEX(number,places)
    Converts an octal number to hexadecimal

Financial Excel Formulas & Functions

1. **AMORDEGRC**
   =AMORDEGRC(cost,date_purchased,first_period,salvage,period,rat
   Returns the depreciation for each accounting period by using a depreciation coefficient
2. **AMORLINC**
   =AMORLINC(cost,date_purchased,first_period,salvage,period,rate,b
   Returns the depreciation for each accounting period
3. **DOLLARDE**
   =DOLLARDE(fractional_dollar,fraction)
   Converts a dollar price, expressed as a fraction, into a dollar price, expressed as a decimal number
4. **DOLLARFR**
   =DOLLARFR(decimal_dollar,fraction)
   Converts a dollar price, expressed as a decimal number, into a

dollar price, expressed as a fraction

5. **SLN**
   =SLN(cost,salvage,life)
   Returns the straight-line depreciation of an asset for one period
6. **SYD**
   =SYD(cost,salvage,life,per)
   Returns the sum-of-years' digits depreciation of an asset for a specified period
7. **DB**
   =DB(cost,salvage,life,period,month)
   Returns the depreciation of an asset for a specified period by using the fixed-declining balance method
8. **DDB**
   =DDB(cost,salvage,life,period,factor)
   Returns the depreciation of an asset for a specified period by using the double-declining balance method or some other method that you specify
9. **EFFECT**
   =EFFECT(nominal_rate,npery)
   Returns the effective annual interest rate
10. **FV**
    =FV(rate,nper,pmt,pv,type)
    Returns the future value of an investment
11. **IPMT**
    =IPMT(rate,per,nper,pv,fv,type)
    Returns the interest payment for an investment for a given period
12. **IRR**
    =IRR(values,guess)
    Returns the internal rate of return for a series of cash flows
13. **MIRR**
    =MIRR(values,finance_rate,reinvest_rate)
    Returns the internal rate of return where positive and negative cash flows are financed at different rates

14. **NOMINAL**
    =NOMINAL(effect_rate,npery)
    Returns the annual nominal interest rate
15. **NPER**
    =NPER(rate,pmt,pv,fv,type)
    Returns the number of periods for an investment
16. **NPV**
    =NPV(rate,value1,value2,...)
    Returns the net present value of an investment based on a series of periodic cash flows and a discount rate
17. **PV**
    =PV(rate,nper,pmt,fv,type)
    Returns the present value of an investment
18. **RATE**
    =RATE(nper,pmt,pv,fv,type,guess)
    Returns the interest rate per period of an annuity
19. **YIELD**
    =YIELD(settlement,maturity,rate,pr,redemption,frequency,basis)
    Returns the yield on a security that pays periodic interest
20. **ACCRINT**
    =ACCRINT(issue,first_interest,settlement,rate,par,frequency,basis,c
    Returns the accrued interest for a security that pays periodic interest
21. **ACCRINTM**
    =ACCRINTM(issue,settlement,rate,par,basis)
    Returns the accrued interest for a security that pays interest at maturity
22. **COUPDAYBS**
    =COUPDAYBS(settlement,maturity,frequency,basis)
    Returns the number of days from the beginning of the coupon period to the settlement date
23. **COUPDAYS**
    =COUPDAYS(settlement,maturity,frequency,basis)
    Returns the number of days in the coupon period that contains the settlement date

24. **COUPDAYSNC**
    =COUPDAYSNC(settlement,maturity,frequency,basis)
    Returns the number of days from the settlement date to the next coupon date
25. **COUPNCD**
    =COUPNCD(settlement,maturity,frequency,basis)
    Returns the next coupon date after the settlement date
26. **COUPNUM**
    =COUPNUM(settlement,maturity,frequency,basis)
    Returns the number of coupons payable between the settlement date and maturity date
27. **COUPPCD**
    =COUPPCD(settlement,maturity,frequency,basis)
    Returns the previous coupon date before the settlement date
28. **CUMIPMT**
    =CUMIPMT(rate,nper,pv,start_period,end_period,type)
    Returns the cumulative interest paid between two periods
29. **CUMPRINC**
    =CUMPRINC(rate,nper,pv,start_period,end_period,type)
    Returns the cumulative principal paid on a loan between two periods
30. **DISC**
    =DISC(settlement,maturity,pr,redemption,basis)
    Returns the discount rate for a security
31. **DURATION**
    =DURATION(settlement,maturity,coupon,yld,frequency,basis)
    Returns the annual duration of a security with periodic interest payments
32. **FVSCHEDULE**
    =FVSCHEDULE(principal,schedule)
    Returns the future value of an initial principal after applying a series of compound interest rates
33. **INTRATE**
    =INTRATE(settlement,maturity,investment,redemption,basis)
    Returns the interest rate for a fully invested security

34. **ISPMT**
    =ISPMT(rate,per,nper,pv)
    Calculates the interest paid during a specific period of an investment
35. **MDURATION**
    =MDURATION(settlement,maturity,coupon,yld,frequency,basis)
    Returns the Macauley modified duration for a security with an assumed par value of $100
36. **ODDFPRICE**
    =ODDFPRICE(settlement,maturity,issue,first_coupon,rate,yld,reden
    Returns the price per $100 face value of a security with an odd first period
37. **ODDFYIELD**
    =ODDFYIELD(settlement,maturity,issue,first_coupon,rate,pr,redem
    Returns the yield of a security with an odd first period
38. **ODDLPRICE**
    =ODDLPRICE(settlement,maturity,last_interest,rate,yld,redemption
    Returns the price per $100 face value of a security with an odd last period
39. **ODDLYIELD**
    =ODDLYIELD(settlement,maturity,last_interest,rate,pr,redemption,
    Returns the yield of a security with an odd last period
40. **PMT**
    =PMT(rate,nper,pv,fv,type)
    Returns the periodic payment for an annuity
41. **PPMT**
    =PPMT(rate,per,nper,pv,fv,type)
    Returns the payment on the principal for an investment for a given period
42. **PRICE**
    =PRICE(settlement,maturity,rate,yld,redemption,frequency,basis)
    Returns the price per $100 face value of a security that pays periodic interest
43. **PRICEDISC**
    =PRICEDISC(settlement,maturity,discount,redemption,basis)

Returns the price per $100 face value of a discounted security

44. **PRICEMAT**
    =PRICEMAT(settlement,maturity,issue,rate,yld,basis)
    Returns the price per $100 face value of a security that pays interest at maturity
45. **RECEIVED**
    =RECEIVED(settlement,maturity,investment,discount,basis)
    Returns the amount received at maturity for a fully invested security
46. **TBILLEQ**
    =TBILLEQ(settlement,maturity,discount)
    Returns the bond-equivalent yield for a Treasury bill
47. **TBILLPRICE**
    =TBILLPRICE(settlement,maturity,discount)
    Returns the price per $100 face value for a Treasury bill
48. **TBILLYIELD**
    =TBILLYIELD(settlement,maturity,pr)
    Returns the yield for a Treasury bill
49. **VDB**
    =VDB(cost,salvage,life,start_period,end_period,factor,no_switch)
    Returns the depreciation of an asset for a specified or partial period by using a declining balance method
50. **XIRR**
    =XIRR(values,dates,guess)
    Returns the internal rate of return for a schedule of cash flows that is not necessarily periodic
51. **XNPV**
    =XNPV(rate,values,dates)
    Returns the net present value for a schedule of cash flows that is not necessarily periodic
52. **YIELDDISC**
    =YIELDDISC(settlement,maturity,pr,redemption,basis)
    Returns the annual yield for a discounted security; for example, a Treasury bill

53. **YIELDMAT**
    =YIELDMAT(settlement,maturity,issue,rate,pr,basis)
    Returns the annual yield of a security that pays interest at maturity

Math and Trigonometry Excel Formulas & Functions

1. **ABS**
   =ABS(number)
   Returns the absolute value of a number
2. **PRODUCT**
   =PRODUCT(number1,number2,...)
   Multiplies its arguments
3. **RAND**
   =RAND()
   Returns a random number between 0 and 1
4. **RANDBETWEEN**
   =RANDBETWEEN(bottom,top)
   Returns a random number between the numbers you specify
5. **ROUND**
   =ROUND(number,num_digits)
   Rounds a number to a specified number of digits
6. **ROUNDDOWN**
   =ROUNDDOWN(number,num_digits)
   Rounds a number down, toward zero
7. **ROUNDUP**
   =ROUNDUP(number,num_digits)
   Rounds a number up, away from zero
8. **SUBTOTAL**
   =SUBTOTAL(function_num,ref1,...)
   Returns a subtotal in a list or database
9. **SUM**
   =SUM(number1,number2,...)
   Adds its arguments

10. **SUMIF**
    =SUMIF(range,criteria,[sum_range])
    Adds the cells specified by a given criteria
11. **SUMIFS**
    =SUMIFS(sum_range,criteria_range,criteria,...)
    Adds the cells in a range that meet multiple criteria
12. **SUMPRODUCT**
    =SUMPRODUCT(array1,array2,[array3],...)
    Returns the sum of the products of corresponding array components
13. **CEILING**
    =CEILING(number,significance)
    Rounds a number to the nearest integer or to the nearest multiple of significance
14. **CEILING.PRECISE**
    =CEILING.PRECISE(number,significance)
    Rounds a number the nearest integer or to the nearest multiple of significance. Regardless of the sign of the number, the number is rounded up.
15. **EVEN**
    =EVEN(number)
    Rounds a number up to the nearest even integer
16. **EXP**
    =EXP(number)
    Returns e raised to the power of a given number
17. **FACT**
    =FACT(number)
    Returns the factorial of a number
18. **FLOOR.PRECISE**
    =FLOOR.PRECISE(number,significance)
    Rounds a number the nearest integer or to the nearest multiple of significance. Regardless of the sign of the number, the number is rounded up.
19. **GCD**
    =GCD(number1,number2,...)

Returns the greatest common divisor

20. **INT**

    =INT(number)

    Rounds a number down to the nearest integer

21. **ISO.CEILING**

    =ISO.CEILING(number,significance)

    Returns a number that is rounded up to the nearest integer or to the nearest multiple of significance

22. **LCM**

    =LCM(number1,number2,...)

    Returns the least common multiple

23. **MOD**

    =MOD(number,divisor)

    Returns the remainder from division

24. **MROUND**

    =MROUND(number,multiple)

    Returns a number rounded to the desired multiple

25. **ODD**

    =ODD(number)

    Rounds a number up to the nearest odd integer

26. **PI**

    =PI()

    Returns the value of pi

27. **POWER**

    =POWER(number,power)

    Returns the result of a number raised to a power

28. **QUOTIENT**

    =QUOTIENT(numerator,denominator)

    Returns the integer portion of a division

29. **SERIESSUM**

    =SERIESSUM(x,n,m,coefficients)

    Returns the sum of a power series based on the formula

30. **SIGN**

    =SIGN(number)

    Returns the sign of a number

31. **SQRT**
    =SQRT(number)
    Returns a positive square root
32. **SUMSQ**
    =SUMSQ(number1,number2,...)
    Returns the sum of the squares of the arguments
33. **TRUNC**
    =TRUNC(number,num_digits)
    Truncates a number to an integer
34. **AGGREGATE**
    =AGGREGATE(function_num,options,array,k)
    Returns an aggregate in a list or database
35. **COMBIN**
    =COMBIN(number,number_chosen)
    Returns the number of combinations for a given number of objects
36. **COS**
    =COS(number)
    Returns the cosine of a number
37. **COSH**
    =COSH(number)
    Returns the hyperbolic cosine of a number
38. **FACTDOUBLE**
    =FACTDOUBLE(number)
    Returns the double factorial of a number
39. **LN**
    =LN(number)
    Returns the natural logarithm of a number
40. **LOG**
    =LOG(number,base)
    Returns the logarithm of a number to a specified base
41. **LOG10**
    =LOG10(number)
    Returns the base-10 logarithm of a number

42. **MULTINOMIAL**
=MULTINOMIAL(number1,number2,...)
Returns the multinomial of a set of numbers
43. **SIN**
=SIN(number)
Returns the sine of the given angle
44. **SINH**
=SINH(number)
Returns the hyperbolic sine of a number
45. **SUMX2MY2**
=SUMX2MY2(array_x,array_y)
Returns the sum of the difference of squares of corresponding values in two arrays
46. **SUMX2PY2**
=SUMX2PY2(array_x,array_y)
Returns the sum of the sum of squares of corresponding values in two arrays
47. **SUMXMY2**
=SUMXMY2(array_x,array_y)
Returns the sum of squares of differences of corresponding values in two arrays
48. **TAN**
=TAN(number)
Returns the tangent of a number
49. **TANH**
=TANH(number)
Returns the hyperbolic tangent of a number
50. **ACOS**
=ACOS(number)
Returns the arccosine of a number
51. **ACOSH**
=ACOSH(number)
Returns the inverse hyperbolic cosine of a number
52. **ASIN**
=ASIN(number)

Returns the arcsine of a number

53. **ASINH**
    =ASINH(number)
    Returns the inverse hyperbolic sine of a number
54. **ATAN**
    =ATAN(number)
    Returns the arctangent of a number
55. **ATAN2**
    =ATAN2(x_num,y_num)
    Returns the arctangent from x- and y-coordinates
56. **ATANH**
    =ATANH(number)
    Returns the inverse hyperbolic tangent of a number
57. **DEGREES**
    =DEGREES(angle)
    Converts radians to degrees
58. **MDETERM**
    =MDETERM(array)
    Returns the matrix determinant of an array
59. **MINVERSE**
    =MINVERSE(array)
    Returns the matrix inverse of an array
60. **MMULT**
    =MMULT(array1,array2)
    Returns the matrix product of two arrays
61. **RADIANS**
    =RADIANS(angle)
    Converts degrees to radians
62. **ROMAN**
    =ROMAN(number,form)
    Converts an arabic numeral to roman, as text
63. **SQRTPI**
    =SQRTPI(number)
    Returns the square root of (number * pi)

Statistical Excel Formulas & Functions

1. **AVERAGE**
   =AVERAGE(number1,number2,...)
   Returns the average of its arguments
2. **AVERAGEIF**
   =AVERAGEIF(range,criteria,[average_range])
   Returns the average (arithmetic mean) of all the cells in a range that meet a given criteria
3. **COUNT**
   =COUNT(value1,value2,...)
   Counts how many numbers are in the list of arguments
4. **COUNTA**
   =COUNTA(value1,value2,...)
   Counts how many values are in the list of arguments
5. **COUNTBLANK**
   =COUNTBLANK(range)
   Counts the number of blank cells within a range
6. **COUNTIF**
   =COUNTIF(range,criteria)
   Counts the number of cells within a range that meet the given criteria
7. **COUNTIFS**
   =COUNTIFS(criteria_range,criteria,...)
   Counts the number of cells within a range that meet multiple criteria
8. **MAX**
   =MAX(number1,number2,...)
   Returns the maximum value in a list of arguments
9. **MEDIAN**
   =MEDIAN(number1,number2,...)
   Returns the median of the given numbers
10. **MIN**
    =MIN(number1,number2,...)
    Returns the minimum value in a list of arguments

11. **TEXT**
    =TEXT(value,format_text)
    Formats a number and converts it to text
12. **AVERAGEA**
    =AVERAGEA(value1,value2,...)
    Returns the average of its arguments, including numbers, text, and logical values
13. **AVERAGEIFS**
    =AVERAGEIFS(average_range,criteria_range,criteria,...)
    Returns the average (arithmetic mean) of all cells that meet multiple criteria
14. **GEOMEAN**
    =GEOMEAN(number1,number2,...)
    Returns the geometric mean
15. **INTERCEPT**
    =INTERCEPT(known_y's,known_x's)
    Returns the intercept of the linear regression line
16. **LARGE**
    =LARGE(array,k)
    Returns the k-th largest value in a data set
17. **LINEST**
    =LINEST(known_y's,known_x's,const,stats)
    Returns the parameters of a linear trend
18. **LOGEST**
    =LOGEST(known_y's,known_x's,const,stats)
    Returns the parameters of an exponential trend
19. **MAXA**
    =MAXA(value1,value2,...)
    Returns the maximum value in a list of arguments, including numbers, text, and logical values
20. **MINA**
    =MINA(value1,value2,...)
    Returns the smallest value in a list of arguments, including numbers, text, and logical values

21. **MODE.MULT**
    =MODE.MULT(number1,number2,...)
    Returns a vertical array of the most frequently occurring, or repetitive values in an array or range of data
22. **MODE.SNGL**
    =MODE.SNGL(number1,number2,...)
    Returns the most common value in a data set
23. **PROB**
    =PROB(x_range,prob_range,lower_limit,upper_limit)
    Returns the probability that values in a range are between two limits
24. **RANK.AVG**
    =RANK.AVG(number,ref,order)
    Returns the rank of a number in a list of numbers
25. **RANK.EQ**
    =RANK.EQ(number,ref,order)
    Returns the rank of a number in a list of numbers
26. **SKEW**
    =SKEW(number1,number2,...)
    Returns the skewness of a distribution
27. **SLOPE**
    =SLOPE(known_y's,known_x's)
    Returns the slope of the linear regression line
28. **SMALL**
    =SMALL(array,k)
    Returns the k-th smallest value in a data set
29. **STANDARDIZE**
    =STANDARDIZE(x,mean,standard_dev)
    Returns a normalized value
30. **TREND**
    =TREND(known_y's,known_x's,new_x's,const)
    Returns values along a linear trend
31. **NORM.S.INV**
    =NORM.S.INV(probability)
    Returns the inverse of the standard normal cumulative

distribution

32. **AVEDEV**
 =AVEDEV(number1,number2,...)
 Returns the average of the absolute deviations of data points from their mean
33. **BETA.DIST**
 =BETA.DIST(x,alpha,beta,cumulative,A,B)
 Returns the beta cumulative distribution function
34. **BETA.INV**
 =BETA.INV(probability,alpha,beta,A,B)
 Returns the inverse of the cumulative distribution function for a specified beta distribution
35. **BINOM.DIST**
 =BINOM.DIST(number_s,trials,probability_s,cumulative)
 Returns the individual term binomial distribution probability
36. **BINOM.INV**
 =BINOM.INV(trials,probability_s,alpha)
 Returns the smallest value for which the cumulative binomial distribution is less than or equal to a criterion value
37. **CHISQ.DIST**
 =CHISQ.DIST(x,deg_freedom,cumulative)
 Returns the cumulative beta probability density function
38. **CHISQ.DIST.RT**
 =CHISQ.DIST.RT(x,deg_freedom)
 Returns the one-tailed probability of the chi-squared distribution
39. **CHISQ.INV**
 =CHISQ.INV(probability,deg_freedom)
 Returns the cumulative beta probability density function
40. **CHISQ.INV.RT**
 =CHISQ.INV.RT(probability,deg_freedom)
 Returns the inverse of the one-tailed probability of the chi-squared distribution
41. **CHISQ.TEST**
 =CHISQ.TEST(actual_range,expected_range)

Returns the test for independence

42. **CONFIDENCE.NORM**
 =CONFIDENCE.NORM(alpha,standard_dev,size)
 Returns the confidence interval for a population mean
43. **CONFIDENCE.T**
 =CONFIDENCE.T(alpha,standard_dev,size)
 Returns the confidence interval for a population mean, using a Student's t distribution
44. **CORREL**
 =CORREL(array1,array2)
 Returns the correlation coefficient between two data sets
45. **COVARIANCE.P**
 =COVARIANCE.P(array1,array2)
 Returns covariance, the average of the products of paired deviations
46. **COVARIANCE.S**
 =COVARIANCE.S(array1,array2)
 Returns the sample covariance, the average of the products deviations for each data point pair in two data sets
47. **DEVSQ**
 =DEVSQ(number1,number2,...)
 Returns the sum of squares of deviations
48. **EXPON.DIST**
 =EXPON.DIST(x,lambda,cumulative)
 Returns the exponential distribution
49. **F.DIST**
 =F.DIST(x,deg_freedom1,deg_freedom2,cumulative)
 Returns the F probability distribution
50. **F.DIST.RT**
 =F.DIST.RT(x,deg_freedom1,deg_freedom2)
 Returns the F probability distribution
51. **F.INV**
 =F.INV(probability,deg_freedom1,deg_freedom2)
 Returns the inverse of the F probability distribution

52. **F.INV.RT**
    =F.INV.RT(probability,deg_freedom1,deg_freedom2)
    Returns the inverse of the F probability distribution
53. **F.TEST**
    =F.TEST(array1,array2)
    Returns the result of an F-test
54. **FISHER**
    =FISHER(x)
    Returns the Fisher transformation
55. **FISHERINV**
    =FISHERINV(y)
    Returns the inverse of the Fisher transformation
56. **FREQUENCY**
    =FREQUENCY(data_array,bins_array)
    Returns a frequency distribution as a vertical array
57. **GAMMA.DIST**
    =GAMMA.DIST(x,alpha,beta,cumulative)
    Returns the gamma distribution
58. **GAMMA.INV**
    =GAMMA.INV(probability,alpha,beta)
    Returns the inverse of the gamma cumulative distribution
59. **GAMMALN**
    =GAMMALN(x)
    Returns the natural logarithm of the gamma function, G(x)
60. **GAMMALN.PRECISE**
    =GAMMALN.PRECISE(x)
    Returns the natural logarithm of the gamma function, G(x)
61. **GROWTH**
    =GROWTH(known_y's,known_x's,new_x's,const)
    Returns values along an exponential trend
62. **HARMEAN**
    =HARMEAN(number1,number2,...)
    Returns the harmonic mean
63. **HYPGEOM.DIST**
    =HYPGEOM.DIST(sample_s,number_sample,population_s,number_po

Returns the hypergeometric distribution

64. **KURT**
    =KURT(number1,number2,...)
    Returns the kurtosis of a data set
65. **LOGNORM.DIST**
    =LOGNORM.DIST(x,mean,standard_dev,cumulative)
    Returns the cumulative lognormal distribution
66. **LOGNORM.INV**
    =LOGNORM.INV(probability,mean,standard_dev)
    Returns the inverse of the lognormal cumulative distribution
67. **NEGBINOM.DIST**
    =NEGBINOM.DIST(number_f,number_s,probability_s,cumulative)
    Returns the negative binomial distribution
68. **NORM.DIST**
    =NORM.DIST(x,mean,standard_dev,cumulative)
    Returns the normal cumulative distribution
69. **NORM.INV**
    =NORM.INV(probability,mean,standard_dev)
    Returns the inverse of the normal cumulative distribution
70. **NORM.S.DIST**
    =NORM.S.DIST(z,cumulative)
    Returns the standard normal cumulative distribution
71. **PEARSON**
    =PEARSON(array1,array2)
    Returns the Pearson product moment correlation coefficient
72. **PERCENTILE.EXC**
    =PERCENTILE.EXC(array,k)
    Returns the k-th percentile of values in a range, where k is in the range 0..1, exclusive
73. **PERCENTILE.INC**
    =PERCENTILE.INC(array,k)
    Returns the k-th percentile of values in a range
74. **PERCENTRANK.EXC**
    =PERCENTRANK.EXC(array,x,significance)
    Returns the rank of a value in a data set as a percentage (0..1,

exclusive) of the data set

75. **PERCENTRANK.INC**
    =PERCENTRANK.INC(array,x,significance)
    Returns the percentage rank of a value in a data set
76. **PERMUT**
    =PERMUT(number,number_chosen)
    Returns the number of permutations for a given number of objects
77. **POISSON.DIST**
    =POISSON.DIST(x,mean,cumulative)
    Returns the Poisson distribution
78. **QUARTILE.EXC**
    =QUARTILE.EXC(array,quart)
    Returns the quartile of the data set, based on percentile values from 0..1, exclusive
79. **QUARTILE.INC**
    =QUARTILE.INC(array,quart)
    Returns the quartile of a data set
80. **RSQ**
    =RSQ(known_y's,known_x's)
    Returns the square of the Pearson product moment correlation coefficient
81. **STDEV.P**
    =STDEV.P(number1,number2,...)
    Calculates standard deviation based on the entire population
82. **STDEV.S**
    =STDEV.S(number1,number2,...)
    Estimates standard deviation based on a sample
83. **STDEVA**
    =STDEVA(value1,value2,...)
    Estimates standard deviation based on a sample, including numbers, text, and logical values
84. **STDEVPA**
    =STDEVPA(value1,value2,...)
    Calculates standard deviation based on the entire population,

including numbers, text, and logical values

85. **STEYX**
    =STEYX(known_y's,known_x's)
    Returns the standard error of the predicted y-value for each x in the regression
86. **T.DIST**
    =T.DIST(x,deg_freedom,cumulative)
    Returns the Percentage Points (probability) for the Student t-distribution
87. **T.DIST.2T**
    =T.DIST.2T(x,deg_freedom)
    Returns the Percentage Points (probability) for the Student t-distribution
88. **T.DIST.RT**
    =T.DIST.RT(x,deg_freedom)
    Returns the Student's t-distribution
89. **T.INV**
    =T.INV(probability,deg_freedom)
    Returns the t-value of the Student's t-distribution as a function of the probability and the degrees of freedom
90. **T.INV.2T**
    =T.INV.2T(probability,deg_freedom)
    Returns the inverse of the Student's t-distribution
91. **T.TEST**
    =T.TEST(array1,array2,tails,type)
    Returns the probability associated with a Student's t-test
92. **TRIMMEAN**
    =TRIMMEAN(array,percent)
    Returns the mean of the interior of a data set
93. **VAR.P**
    =VAR.P(number1,number2,...)
    Calculates variance based on the entire population
94. **VAR.S**
    =VAR.S(number1,number2,...)
    Estimates variance based on a sample

95. **VARA**
    =VARA(value1,value2,...)
    Estimates variance based on a sample, including numbers, text, and logical values
96. **VARPA**
    =VARPA(value1,value2,...)
    Calculates variance based on the entire population, including numbers, text, and logical values
97. **WEIBULL.DIST**
    =WEIBULL.DIST(x,alpha,beta,cumulative)
    Returns the Weibull distribution
98. **Z.TEST**
    =Z.TEST(array,x,sigma)
    Returns the one-tailed probability-value of a z-test

Printed by Libri Plureos GmbH in Hamburg,
Germany